BARROW STEELWORKS
The Open Hearth Years 1880 - 1959

An Illustrated History

Cover Illustrations
Back Page: Tapping the fire; K.Royall, Looking across Walney Channel; John Duffin, No.3 Hoop Mill; D.Howden

The Works in 1880
"A monster iron-mining-smelting company..."
Punch, 1867

"It was assumed that like Black Combe in the background, it would stand forever"
Barrow Steelworks, 2015

Courtesy of Geoff Berry
(inspired by the plinth of the Ramsden monument, Barrow-in-Furness)

BARROW STEELWORKS
The Open Hearth Years 1880 - 1959
An Illustrated History

STAN HENDERSON AND KEN ROYALL

Published by Henderson & Royall 2017

© Henderson & Royall

Book interior & Cover Design by Russell Holden
www.pixeltweakspublications.com

Printed by Ingram

ISBN: 978-0-9956190-5-0

Contents

Introduction... 1

The Main Man (a biographical note)..................... 5

Chapter 1: 1880 – 1918 9
Chapter 2: The Inter-War Years 18
Chapter 3: 1942 and United Steel 34
Chapter 4: The Siemens Labratory 42
Chapter 5: Products 45

Appendix 1
Some More Key Personnel Over the Years 56

Appendix 2
The Board of Directors 59

Appendix 3... 65

Bibliography.. 83

The Hindpool Main Line

Courtesy of Michael Andrews, Geoff Holme collection (Mac 123)

This railroad cut right through the Hindpool works in fact it pre-dated the steelworks – being laid in 1860. In the early days it hindered the transporting of molten iron from the blast furnaces to the Bessemers and although an engineering solution was possible, Mr Smith, the first manager chose not to pursue it. Looking from left to right we see the blast furnaces then the incline planes leading down to the charging depots. We see a sandstone retaining wall, in the distance is the zigzag gas main, then the chimney and western edge of the marine boiler house. (The south-bound engine was running light, April, 1955)

(On his own admission Andrew Carnegie said that he modelled his new works, the Edgar Thomson Steelworks in Pittsburgh, PA., USA on Barrow. Even, as with Barrow, being bisected by a main railroad, the Baltimore and Ohio Railway)

Acknowledgements

This book is a companion volume to *Barrow Steelworks – An illustrated History*, 2015. It is based largely on personal communications and traditional knowledge passed down by retired steel workers, most notable being the late Bill Pearson.

The authors would acknowledge the important role played by the *North Western Evening Mail* and its sister paper the *Barrow News* who, over the decades, have chronicled the vicissitudes of the Barrow Company. Acknowledgements are made to Archivist Susan Benson and the staff of Cumbria Archives and Local Studies Centre (Barrow), Sabine Skae of the Dock Museum also Bill Myers. Many of the photographs used, were taken by K. E. Royall, manager of the fuel and instrument department, also works photographer from 1957, or sourced from his extensive collection. Every attempt has been made to contact copyright holders. 12 x 10 plate negatives now reside at the Dock Museum.

A bibliography of works consulted is included to give the reader the opportunity for further reading.

Introduction

It is difficult from our present standpoint to appreciate the immense size the works had once been, even by 19th century standards, it made other works look positively Lilliputian. It had been estimated in one quarter to have left the German concern Krupp far behind. It was also, according to local historian J.D. Marshall, the most successful company of its kind – in that it could pay a dividend of 20% for eleven years. Barrow had been the show works of the world and one time largest employer in Cumberland and North Lancashire. It had been the model used by the great Andrew Carnegie in building his own steel empire in the United States. At Barrow the heady days of 'empire' were numbered, there were clear signs that the heavily exploited iron ore deposits were becoming impoverished.

The year 1880 was a pivotal year for the Steel Company, indeed the decade would be one of change and frustration. J. T. Smith had just completed a re-modelling of the Bessemer plant (and then seven years later would retire), in removing the converter vessels and hammers from the northern end of No.3 shed he had made space for the new open hearth furnaces. Throughout the decade Barrow still remained one of the Bessemer strongholds, although open hearth steelmaking would become the main process at the works until 1959. Without doubt and more significant would be the arrival of the basic method of steelmaking, developed by 'amateur' metallurgist Sidney Gilchrist Thomas. This was initially adopted more on the Continent than here in Britain, however it would soon become one of several factors that ended the lucrative position that Barrow works, or more to the point, the directors and shareholders, had enjoyed for many years. (Dividends dropped to 5% and yet in 1881 the works manufactured a record 4,630 tons of steel, the largest amount ever produced in one week by a single firm). Inferior ores containing a proportion of phosphorous and sulphur could now be used, both here and abroad.

The entrance to the Barcon offices 1962. The slate murals depicting the three steelmaking processes used can be seen. These murals, part of Barrow's steel heritage, now reside in a part of Barrow town hall (2016) inaccessible to the public.

The death of the patriarch, Henry Schneider, in 1887 left everyone reeling. Following his death the *Barrow News* reported that during his lifetime Schneider had given nearly £70,000 for the erection of civic amenities.

The expected upsurge following the Great War never happened, in fact there was a nationwide slump in the iron and steel industry. During this period Barrow embarked on a post-war reconstruction programme. The re-modelled open hearth plant would remain unchanged, apart from matters of detail, until 1959.

As with Workington iron and steelworks Barrow was saved by coming under the control of the Sheffield based United Steel Companies.

At the conception stage of *'Barrow Steelworks'*, Ken Royall and I agreed that part of our rationale in determining the book's justification was to record Barrow's achievement regarding continuous casting during the 1950s. (Covered in some detail in *Barrow Steelworks*, 2015). It was totally unacceptable to us that virtually nothing existed in the town to mark this important milestone in the history of steel production. The only reference, found in Barrow's Dock Museum (thankfully now removed) was a notice, a kind of footnote to a narrative about the town's Bessemer past, which read – *'During the 1950s other production methods were tried, but the works eventually closed in 1983'.* These 'other production methods', were to revolutionise steelmaking globally making the orthodox ingots obsolete. Barrow was chosen to run with this experimental work for one reason, cited by scientist Iain Halliday at the first meeting of the Continuous

Casting Steering Committee, "Barrow could proceed from a sound basis of know-how and intelligent experience developed over seventy years". During the research for the book I asked my father – who had worked for fifteen years in the process – why he thought the invention did not receive more recognition. He told me that whilst it was certainly a big event in the steel world, unlike the town's other heavy industry – shipbuilding – the end product of a steel mill is not glamorous, unlike a ship launch where dignitaries in their finery would gather with pomp and ceremony and children gleefully waved their union flags. Additionally, he said, you need to look at what else was going on in the world around the same time that may have overshadowed events at Barrow Steelworks. Locally we had the launch of England's largest passenger liner Oriana (1959), in 1960 there was the launch of Britain's first nuclear powered submarine Dreadnought. Internationally there was the development of the Laser in 1960 and then the first man into outer space – Yuri Gagarin, 1961. Certainly enough to occupy the imagination of the man, or woman in the street.

This book aims to focus on the open hearth years, the actual process as used at Barrow and the main changes the works underwent together with some of the personnel involved in taking the works forward into the middle of the 20th century.

An appendix is included which contains miscellaneous items, previously unseen photos along with personal reminiscences. *S. Henderson, 2016*

The visitor waiting room inside Barcon.
Mounted on the wood-panelled wall is a slate mural depicting the early years of the works.
This, along with the three in the top photo, were placed with Barrow Council following the works demolition in 1984.

1866

The Main Man
(a biographical note)

During the second part of the Industrial Revolution, in 1839 to be precise, a London businessman came to the Lake District on holiday. During his sojourn he met with a James Jopling who was the Furness advisor to the Earl of Burlington and also involved with the management of the Earl's slate quarries at Kirkby-in-Furness. The *offcomer's* name was Henry William Schneider (1817 – 1887) and his family's business was principally that of mineral exploration, precious metals also tin and copper both here and abroad. (Little did he know at the time but he was soon to become heavily involved with the master metal – iron and the romance of steel).

Schneider lived and travelled in a lavish style and was in a league above the other Furness ore merchants.

Jopling told Schneider of his belief that rich deposits of iron ore lay beneath Burlington's land at Park, to the south of Askam-in-Furness. As a result of this conversation Schneider leased mining rights on the Park Farm estate. His efforts were to prove unrewarding. He took a partner, one James Davis, eventually forming the Furness Mining Company and after more disappointments and heavy outlay they purchased established mines in the royalty of the Duke of Buccleuch who was Lord of the Manor of Furness. These mines, Mouzell and Whitriggs, lay to the north-east of Dalton-in-Furness and provided good business. The partnership established a *floor* on the Strand in Barrow in an area now occupied by the Harbour public house, they also erected a jetty into Barrow Channel for the loading of their ironstone.

From the outset Schneider had been aware of the lack of a transport system for moving the ore to the embarkation points sited along the Furness coastline. The other ore merchants prevailed upon him to use what influence he had to have a tramway constructed. He approached Burlington for a loan of £40,000 for such a purpose.

Nothing came of the request. This would later fall to Burlington and eventually both he and Buccleuch put up equal amounts towards establishing the Furness Railway. (Schneider never did become embroiled in the machinations of the Furness Railway Company).

It would be a decade later, in 1850, when the royalty was due to lapse, that Burlington himself persuaded Schneider to make one last effort to find iron at Park. Schneider's last desperate attempt was again proving fruitless and he was on the verge of abandoning the project as the allocated funds were all but used up. What happened next led to a series of events that guaranteed him a place in the history of the aforementioned Industrial Revolution. Schneider was approached by a spokesman for his men who were offering to work for one more week without pay in the hope of making a strike. (He had been a good employer, relative to the standards of the time, his men obviously acknowledging the fact). A shaft was sunk not far from the original attempt and at a depth of about 36 feet a large deposit of iron ore was struck. This strike was to be the largest find in British history up to that time. Later named the Burlington pit, it was to yield over nine million tons of haematite. Shortly after the discovery, Davis terminated the partnership obviously unaware of the extent of the strike. He later became known as the man who was 'always in the right place at the wrong time', for six years later he would also exclude himself from the even bigger find at Hodbarrow near Millom, Cumberland.

Following Davis' departure Schneider took a new partner – one Robert Hannay, a wealthy land owner from Kirkudbrightshire, Scotland. On 1st January, 1853 they formed Schneider, Hannay and Company. Up to this point Schneider had commuted between Furness and his home in London, now due to the sheer size of his interests in Furness he moved into the area purchasing Swarthdale then later taking Lightburn House, both in Ulverston. Up to twenty domestic servants would pander to his needs.

Although said to have been arrogant and opinionated he gave willingly of his time and money (but not anonymously it must be said), he sat on numerous committees, was a magistrate, Barrow's third mayor, guardian of the poor and a staunch churchman. Following his death while resident at Belsfield in Bowness, the *Barrow News* reported that he gave almost £70,000 (more than one million today) for the erection of civic amenities. And although not exactly a Titus Salt, he had gained the tag, 'the most generous and liberal despot in Lancashire'.

Henry Schneider
'Steel Man', Ironmaster and Industrialist.
Courtesy of A. G. Banks

1

1880 – 1918

The open hearth steelmaking process was based on the work of Sir William Siemens, a German engineer, who later became a British subject. Siemens came to the north of England twice, once in 1846 and then later in 1874 when he spoke at the dinner given to the Iron and Steel Institute in Barrow. – "It was", he said, "in the year 1846 that I visited the district from across the seas, and that beautiful ruin Furness Abbey. At that time I had heard that there was a village called Barrow – a village of, perhaps, 300 inhabitants – but all the signs I could see of iron smelting were a few tip-forges and an old tip where puddling ore was shot occasionally. . ."

Sir William Siemens, 1823-1883
Courtesy of W. MacFarlane.

Josiah Timmis Smith, 1823-1906

Siemens applied the regenerative principle to the reverberatory furnace (developed in the eighteenth century by Henry Cort for his Puddling Process) whereby a honeycomb of fire bricks, called the checkers, (also referred to as chequers), beneath the hearth absorbs heat from the waste gases and then returns it to the incoming gases in an alternating cycle. This method could save up to 75% of the fuel previously used. Together with Frenchman Pierre Martin, who proposed the diluting of the pig iron with scrap wrought iron, they developed what became generally known as the Siemens-Martin Open Hearth Process. The early furnaces were fuelled by coal fires, these fires were sited at each end of the furnace but this arrangement often led to problems with the hot air flows causing clinkering of the ash with heavy wear of the fire bed. Siemens overcame this problem by inventing the gas producer which took the fire and all solid fuel right away from the furnace and the checkers. It was this improved open hearth furnace model that Barrow bought into.

The open hearth plant at Barrow was launched on a modest scale compared to the Bessemer operation and was the last major project overseen by Smith – who had just been made President of the Iron and Steel Institute. Josiah Timmis Smith was born at Duckmanton lodge near Chesterfield, he came from a family with a long association with the industry. Upon completing his education he went to the Dundyvan works to learn blast furnace management. He later went into partnership with his father running the Duckmanton ironworks. Around 1850 he spent nearly one year at Le Creusot, a 'state-of-the-art', ironworks in eastern France. He was, therefore, an experienced ironmaster prior to making the acquaintance of Messrs Schneider and Hannay.

The town's population had just edged 50,000 when, in 1880, two 12-ton furnaces were erected, together with the necessary gas producers, towards the northern end of No.3 shed in an area previously occupied by steam hammers. Smith so arranged his plant to receive either molten blast furnace metal or partially blown metal from the converters. This was a relatively new departure at the time known as the Duplex system, it obviated the need for the cupolas - normally associated with this type of plant. Adopting the open hearth process would be a tactical move in light of the emergence of the basic method of steelmaking. It allowed Barrow to diversify while retaining the Bessemers on acid steelmaking. (Bessemer steel was always slightly higher in nitrogen compared with other types of steels. For some purposes, notably railway lines, this was advantageous). It was also one step towards making the steelmaking side of the works independent of the ironworks.

In August, 1880 the Institution of Mechanical Engineers came to the town again. They were received and provided with a luncheon by the Mayor, Edward Wadham, Esq and were to spend the week inspecting most of Barrow's main industries starting with the docks and the Barrow Shipbuilding Works. Later in the week they were escorted to the works of the Barrow Haematite Steel Company where members reported witnessing ingot casting under steam pressure. The Authors could not reconcile this statement with what was known about ingot casting at Barrow. It is concluded that what the members actually witnessed was ingot stripping. Towards the end of the nineteenth century Barrow works had a more sophisticated mechanical stripping plant than it had during the 1950s. (A pioneer works can obviously slip back in some regards!).

Open hearth steel was initially used in the three steel foundries, also the ingot mould foundry (which also worked in haematite iron) sited at the north end of the works.

The men of the old ingot mould foundry, 1890.

The ingot mould foundry was a brick building 150 feet long and 60 feet wide sited near to the works boundary wall on Walney Road, directly opposite the entrance to the North Lancashire Brick Works (in 2016 a retail park). This foundry had its own cupola for melting haematite iron. It made a variety of ingot moulds, covers for converter bottoms and slag tubs. Within ten years it was closed with the work being outsourced to the David Caird foundry on Hindpool Road. (See appendices).

The works canteen, left, with the old ingot mould foundry far right, 17th June, 1977.

No.1 steel foundry was located to the north of No.2 steel shed. This brick building, which also had its own cupola, became the boiler shop in later years. No.2 foundry was an extension to the northern end of No.3 steel shed. This foundry aligned the Siemens casting pit and was referred to as the north-end casting pit. (Many years later it would become the home of the experimental continuous casting pilot plant). No.3 foundry was immediately south of the Siemens furnaces, the area would later become the Siemens laboratory and offices.

Late in the afternoon on the 26th of February, 1887 hydraulic crane operator John Bowman, aged 60, of Vernon Street, Hindpool had just started his shift on the Siemens pit. He was preparing to place a group of 2-ton ingot moulds into the casting pit. At the same time a steam loco pulling wagons started moving down the bay. There was a sudden metallic crash and bang and the ingot moulds started toppling, trapping Bowman. Pitman John Becket of Dundonald Street, Hindpool saw the accident and summoned help. While being pulled clear by workmates he was heard to mutter that his legs hurt. On arrival at hospital he was found to have fractures to both legs with widespread contusions to his body. He died the next morning. The inquest heard that a locomotive coming into the Siemens casting bay had collided with a long piece of scrap metal that was lying across the top of the moulds causing them to fall. *The Barrow Herald* of Saturday, March 1st carried a report of the accident. Apart from being potentially dangerous some parts of the works were not conducive to good health. In some areas men were breathing air that would have stunted an oak tree –

hence the many reported cases of pneumonia and bronchitis. Less than two weeks later, on March, 12th 1887, the *Herald* again reported that William the 7th Duke of Devonshire and chairman of the Company had retired due to advancing years and failing health. The Duke who was in his 80th year had appointed his eldest son, the Marquis of Hartington, as his successor.

Also in the year Josiah Smith, general manager, announced his retirement then on the 11th November founding father Henry Schneider passed away at his home at Bowness on Windermere.

By 1891 the open hearth plant had grown to eight furnaces, three being basic, and the others acid (See diagram on p.17). The furnaces were arranged in two banks of four each side of the casting pit which ran down the centre of No.3 shed. Open hearth steel was used for ships' plate, tube manufacture and a variety of steel castings for marine and ordnance purposes.

The company had always been careful to proceed by experiment in most of the work that they had undertaken, and they conferred great benefits on the trade, and on rail users generally, by researches they made in different directions to determine the qualities of steel manufactured under different conditions. Perhaps the most important of these was that undertaken between 1865 and 1875, and, of which the results were communicated to the Institution of Civil Engineers in the latter year. These experiments were about, if not quite, the first to determine the effects of increased hardness, heavy traffic, molecular tension etc. The results of another

A group of ingot moulds on a chariot. *Courtesy of British Steel.*

13

important series of tests and experiments made by the company was at a later date communicated to the Iron and Steel Institute. These tests were carried out on the company's Kirkcaldy testing machine – one of the first erected at a private steelworks. It was also via experiment that Barrow determined that the initial Bessemer blow used in the Duplex process could be satisfactorily achieved with oxygen in a ladle, rendering the converter and associated blower plant unnecessary.

Cupolas are basically scaled-down versions of the blast furnace, known at Barrow as baby furnaces they were deployed across the site. A cupola comprised a cylindrical tower of steel plate, lined with fire bricks and supplied with a soft cold blast through a series of tuyeres. The blower on the smaller furnaces was usually just a fan but larger types were supplied from a positive displacement blower. It was patented in 1794 by 18th century Cumbrian ironmaster John Wilkinson.

Marine casting in No.1 steel foundry awaiting shipment
This is an example of an application where haematite steel is superior to haematite iron.
(from a 12 x 10 plate neg)

Cupolas only operate intermittently as they have no water cooling system and the refractory lining is well worn by the end of a day's work. The bottom is made to drop open so that the contents can be cleared easily. Cupolas vary in size from about 18 inches internal diameter up to some 10 feet or so. In the 1890s Barrow's Bessemer shop had four cupolas for melting Spiegel and pig iron.

The last general manager of the 19th century was Mr J.M.While. James Morgan While came from Glamorganshire and had a long and varied experience at Dowlais, Ebbw Vale, Darlington and elsewhere in the management of steelworks. He started at Barrow works in 1891. During his tenure he was responsible for a number of mechanical improvements, including the complete re-modelling of the Bessemer plant, which increased the general efficiency and economy of working. He lived with his family at Whinsfield and they had two servant girls. Whinsfield was a sandstone mansion, owned by the company, at the top of Cocken Road, due north of the works (see p.70).

Mr J. M. While. Director, in his 60th year. *Courtesy of Cumbria Archives & local studies centre*

In September, 1903 the autumn meeting of the Iron and Steel Institute convened in Barrow for the second time with its new chairman, Andrew Carnegie, (previous incumbents included William, 7th Duke of Devonshire; Sir Henry Bessemer; Sir William Siemens and Josiah Timmis Smith). The visit, lasting from the 1st to the 4th of the month, included a tour of several mines and other industrial concerns in the district. The elaborate programme was planned and co-ordinated by Mr A. Butchart in his capacity of executive committee secretary. Barrow council marked the occasion by decorating the streets and interiors of municipal buildings. By 11am on the first day a large crowd had congregated outside the town hall where the mayor and council members had gathered to welcome the dignitaries. The visitors who had

Mr A. Butchart. Courteous and able Company Secretary. *Courtesy of NW. Evening Mail*

15

arrived by rail, were first taken around the works of the Furness Railway Company. Credit for the smooth running of the event going to the work's courteous and able secretary, Andrew Butchart. In his address Dr Carnegie – who referred to Barrow as 'the cradle of the Institute' – made reference to the growth of the town since his first visit twenty-nine years previous, commenting, among other things on the spacious avenues (Abbey Road) lined with trees, the statues of the founding fathers; free library and technical school also the working mens club. (Aka *'The House of Lords'* and destroyed by fire in 2017). The progress was, he said, something of which all Barrow people could be proud.

The years preceding the First World War were a very quiet period and marked what could be termed the beginning of the 'dark ages' – if one were to liken the era to that period in classical history. The year 1908 was a particularly bad year for stop and start closures. On Saturday the 11th of January, the *Barrow Herald* reported – 'Better Prospects for Hindpool' in that from Monday the 13th all departments, excluding the merchant mill, would resume normal operations. Later that week the paper reported that the Steelworks Band were to give a series of concerts at Barrow's Hippodrome – as if to almost celebrate the news! The news would have a hollow ring for in the March, the same week that the *Herald* reported the death of the 8th Duke of Devonshire, James While announced that for want of orders the works were facing a three months stoppage. Mr While had just been appointed to the position of director by a vote of the Board

With the start of the First World War the UK steel industry was slow to rally in support. With the Shell Crisis of 1915, where there was much public and media criticism, the industry was mobilised by the newly formed Ministry of Munitions. Whereas, in early 1914 there had been a significant falling-off of the already depressed iron trade, the war once again meant 'business as usual' for Barrow works. During the first half of 1917, 199,008-tons of iron ore passed through Barrow Docks. The works went, almost, back into full employment.

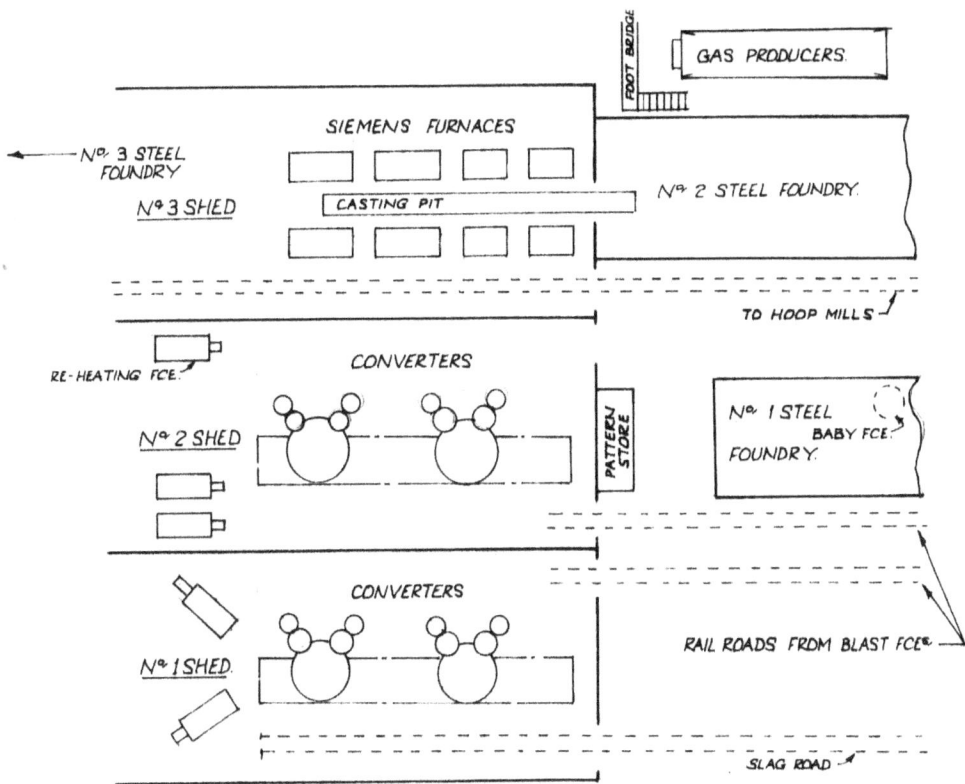

Layout of steelmaking plant in 1891. Per: *Iron & Coal Trades Review*, 1899.

1910 and three senior managers, in bow ties, surrounded by department heads.
Middle row, 4th from left is Mr J. M. While just before his retirement.

2

The Inter-War Years

The period immediately after the end of the First World War saw a dramatic drop in the number of employees at the Hindpool works, down to around 1,200. Much of the reduction was due to natural wastage as folk left the town for pastures new. Several factors now influenced decisions taken at the works, apart from the national position i.e. the general slump in the industry exacerbated by the national coal strike of 1921. Output of UK steel fell by over 55%. Locally the directors were faced with the fact that iron ore reserves in Furness were all but exhausted and what did remain was becoming more and more expensive to mine due to flooding of the mines. Orders for steel rails from developing countries had fallen away and the works had lost the Belfast shipyard orders to cheaper American steel. (Although the 1920s saw a marked decline in shipbuilding). *The Barrow and District Year Book* called 1921 'a black year', a description that goes hand in hand with the epithet 'dark ages' alluded to in the previous chapter.

View of the works from the south in the early 1920s, there appears to be adequate rail stock in the marshalling areas. The pedestrians in the foreground were plying betwee Hindpool Road and the underpass that led to Ironworks Road. *12 x 10 plate neg*

In 1919 it was agreed by the Board that Bessemer steelmaking would cease with investment for the future directed, firstly, at the hoop works. During 1917 a feasibility study was done looking into the electrification of No's 1 and 2 mills. And then the installation of two new bar mills (Double Duo). In the main steelworks an upgrade of the open hearth plant was undertaken; additionally, the Cornish boiler plant was replaced with the more efficient Lancashire model. The directors obviously adopting Carnegie's philosophy – "the best time to expand is when no-one else dare take the risks".

Works management in 1922, photographed outside the gas engine house
L to R: H. Roberts, Siemens dept. manager; E. Repton, steelworks manager; G. Machin, traffic manager; P. List, general manager; A. Timmins, foundry manager; T. Prosser, chief draughtsman; F. Bowker, chief chemist; J. Clements, chief engineer; J. Danks, ironworks manager; J. Seddon, building dept. manager; J. Timms, rail bank manager.
On the left is the works limousine with chauffeur, J.Thistlethwaite. *Courtesy of L. Roach.*

The chairman of the Company was now one G. Muir Ritchie, for the first time the works were without ducal influence. The general manager, Francis Paul List, was born in Luxembourg which itself boasted a thriving steel industry. Prior to taking up his new position Mr List had been the Luxembourg consul to Barrow.

The first works undertaken as part of the project was the installation of the new gas producing machines. These were sited to the west of the new Siemens scrap gantry immediately south of the wrought iron footbridge which linked the two main sections of the works. This battery of Morgan gas producers would eventually supplant the 72 smaller units which were to the south of the steel sheds. All early open hearth (O.A.)

Francis P. List, BSc. General Manager of the inter-war years.

William Killingbeck, the last general manager of the entire iron and steel complex. *Courtesy of NW. Evening Mail*

furnaces were fuelled with producer gas, which was an inflammable gas generated by passing a blast of air and steam up through a deep bed of red hot, low sulphur, coal. The operation of the gas machine is continuous, fresh coal entering the top and ash being shovelled out from the bottom. The walls and top of the producers were cooled by means of water jackets. The water boiled in the top jacket and so provided the steam for the blast.

The volume of the blast and the air/steam ratio were controlled automatically. The chemical reactions that took place in the process were very similar to those in a blast furnace.

Interior view of the Morgan gas producers showing the coal hoppers, circa 1923. 12 x 10 plate neg.

A group of labourers working on the boilers in 1920, these men are actually sat on the Stirling boilers. Front row right is 19 years old Harry Goodwin of Lancaster Street, Barrow. *Courtesy of D. Goodwin.*

The labourers on the west side of the works, on the boilers and in the stock yards and marshalling areas were under the control of gangers. These men, like the blast furnace managers, could be hard-nosed bullies not opposed to knocking a man down if they believed such action was appropriate in controlling matters within their fiefdom. And like the bowler-hatted trade head foremen over at the shipyard, had the power of hire and fire. These gangers also paid out the workmen in their charge, for many years at the premises behind the *Black Boy* public house on the corner of Blake Street and Calcutta Street, which was used as a pay-office. (Years later it would become Whittall's fish and chip shop).

With most of the ancillary work completed alterations to the melting shop were undertaken leaving the actual reconstruction of the furnaces till last. The overhead crane rails were raised to 37 feet above ground level to ensure adequate clearance above the larger furnaces. The remodelled melting shop would be in two 55 feet wide bays and extend 400 feet along No.3 steel shed.

Front view of Stirling boilers. *Courtesy of W. MacFarlane*

21

Around this period 87% of UK steel was coming from O.H. furnaces. Since the First World War scrap steel gradually became one of the most important raw materials in the British economy. The fact that the O.H. process could consume scrap was an attractive feature. At Barrow it broke the dependence on the blast furnaces. Over the LMS goods line the ironworks had carved something of a niche with the export of its s.p. pig iron. This was an area where, following a close study of customer requirements, it had been recognised that a percentage of phosphorous was desirable in irons used for the manufacture of certain castings. Research also revealed that castings with over 0.35% phosphorous frequently suffered from porosity and general weakness. (A condition known as *cold-shortness*).

Britain became a scrap-importing nation, ships which went out loaded with coal often returned with a cargo of scrap steel.

Open hearth furnaces were either fixed (static) or of the tilting variety. They came in a range of sizes from, say 15-tons to 300-tons capacity. Fixed furnaces were the choice at Barrow as the tilting models, with their deeper hearths, were more suitable for use with hot metal charges. They were also more costly to build and could not melt the entire charge from the solid state. Eight furnaces were erected to replace the older,

Northern-end of the new 200 yards long Siemens scrap gantry which carried overhead electro-magnetic cranes. .

Aerial view, looking east, 1920s. K. Norman collection.

smaller units. There were three at 80-tons (1, 2 and 3); four at 45-tons (E, F, G and H and one at 15-tons capacity. The complete battery of furnaces were erected in a line along the west side of the casting pit. A large steel platform was constructed at the front side which was from where the furnaces were managed and charged. The smaller O.H. furnaces were on a different level from the 80-ton units, a step of about four feet separating the two sections. Below the platform were the checkers and reversing valves. These valves, a kind of four-way butterfly valve, had extended spindles up through the platform to a position close to the furnace crew's shelter (see drawing on page 24). The reversing valves controlled the flow and contra-flow of the air and gases, which had to be reversed every 15 to 20 minutes.

At Barrow each furnace ran with a crew of four men, a leading hand (the melter), a second and third hand also a utility man. The shop had a potential of 4,000 ingot tons per week.

The crew of F furnace, one of the 40-ton units, l to r Les Jones, leading hand John Thompson; unknown, unknown. 3rd March, 1953

23

SECTION THROUGH WORKS LOOKING NORTH

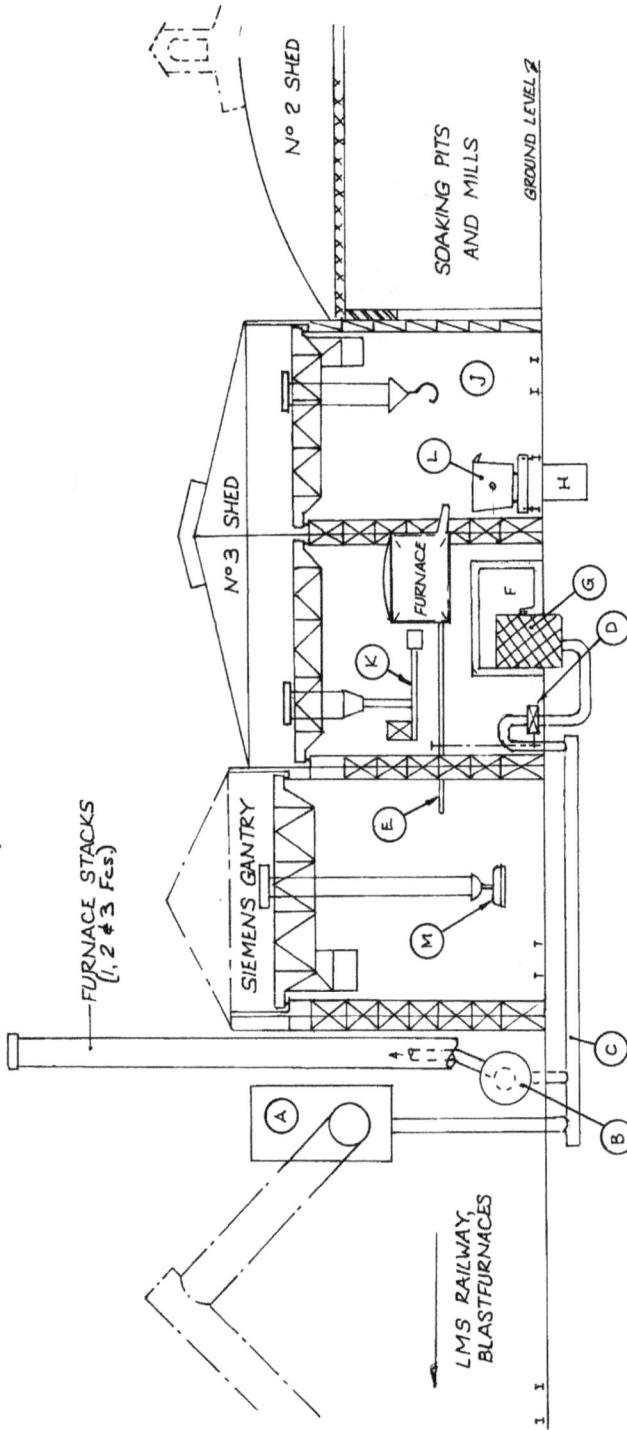

(NOT TO SCALE)

No 2 SHED

SOAKING PITS
AND MILLS

GROUND LEVEL 2

No 3 SHED

FURNACE

J

L

H

K

F

G

D

E

M

SIEMENS GANTRY

FURNACE STACKS
(1, 2 & 3 Fcs)

LMS RAILWAY
BLASTFURNACES

A

B

C

Main Elements

A = Gas Producers

B = Waste Heat Boiler

C = Gas Culvert

D = Reversing Valves

E = charging platform

F = Slag Pocket

G = Checkers

H = Casting Pit

J = Ingot Stripping Area

K = Wellman Charger

L = Ladle

M = Magnet

S. HENDERSON

24

Open hearth steelmaking comprised three distinct stages:-

1. The charging period, during which the cold metal charge together with the slag forming constituents were loaded into the hearth. The arrangement for doing this, unlike the pre-war *modus operandi*, was via a mechanical charger. This charger was suspended from the cross-travel of an overhead crane (see below). Manual charging had been hot exhausting work and took much longer. The materials to be charged were placed in long narrow boxes called pans, each pan capable of holding about 2-tons. The pans were of steel plate construction with a casting fixed to one end which the *peel* of the charger could latch onto. The contents of each pan would be carefully inspected, weighed and recorded for costing purposes. Mr Curnick, the department manager, needed to know exactly what and how much went into his furnaces. When full the charging pans were placed on the ledge of the platform by the stockyard men ready for the charger. The peel of the charger would clamp on and would be swung through 180 degrees depositing the contents into the appropriate furnace by its centre working door.

2. The melting period, during which the contents of the furnace became molten and separated out into molten metal and molten slag.

The front-side and a 5-ton Wellman charger empties its pan into one of the furnaces. (BHS.Co. Ltd.)

With his furnace 'opened-out', the leading hand (melter) keeps a watchful eye on the process. 12 x 10 plate neg.

During this part of this process the furnace would be 'opened out', i.e. made to burn fuel at the fastest rate, without endangering the furnace roof – which had temperature monitoring points fitted. The idea being to get the charge molten as soon as possible. By the time it was ready for refining all the silicon, manganese and sulphur (in basic furnaces) should have been oxidised out of the metal. The flow of air and gases was alternated every 20 minutes or so, the reversing valves being changed over in response to an indicator light on the control panel. The melter kept a careful eye on the slag to make sure it had formed properly, he could then be sure, before removing the carbon that all the other undesirable elements were out of harm's way in the slag.

Close-up view of a furnace being charged by one of the mechanical chargers. 22nd Feb 1956.

3. The refining period, the final phase of O.H. steelmaking where the last of the carbon was removed. At Barrow the term was to 'boil down the bath', (because the carbon came out as carbon monoxide gas) bubbles appeared all over the surface of the molten pool giving the appearance of a boiling liquid. Open hearth steel contained anything from 0.06% to 0.8% of carbon. The process had the advantage over the Bessemer converter in being much more controllable, steels of practically any carbon content could be made. At regular intervals during the boil the leading hand inserted a small iron spoon and took metal samples which he poured into an iron mould. From the appearance of the fracture when the sample had been broken an assessment of the carbon content could be made, this was then verified by chemical analysis. Open hearth heats were finished off in one of two ways at Barrow. In one the carbon was 'boiled' right down to an absolute minimum. Haematite pig iron was then thrown into the bath – referred to as 'pigging back'. The carbon in the pig absorbed the excess iron oxide then raised the carbon content to its required level. In the other method the carbon was 'caught' at the required level by stopping the boil, this was done by adding Ferro-silicon, an alloy of iron and silicon which contained little or no carbon. This method was used when making a high carbon steel where pigging back would be unsatisfactory. Ferro manganese, in small amounts, was also occasionally added prior to tapping.

Subject to final chemical analysis, verified by a senior chemist the furnace was ready for tapping. The tap hole was opened with a hammer and crow bar, it was also poked from inside using a long bar pushed over the sill of the middle door. Molten metal ran out first followed by a flush of slag. To stop too much slag coming over into the ladle the furnace launder was adjusted to deflect the slag into a tub or the pit below the furnace, O.H. slag tended to damage the ladle lining. It was essential that the furnace was fully drained of metal, any pools of steel left on the hearth would be oxidised during the next charging damaging the furnace lining. The furnacemen would 'rabble' the hearth absolutely clean prior to fettling. Before charging for the next heat could begin the 2nd hand would make up the tap hole (tap to tap time at Barrow was between 7 and 12 hours).

Slag being diverted into an alongside tub during the tapping of an open hearth furnace. 22nd Feb 1956.

From tapping, the steel was handed over to the men on the 'back side', known as the pit men and teemers who would commence ingot casting.

The furnace had been emptied into a large fire brick lined container called a Bessemer ladle (so called because it was originally designed for use with Bessemer steel). The ladle sat on a four wheel bogey which moved on wheels and so straddled the Siemens pit.

Ladles used at Barrow were equipped with two nozzles so that two ingots could be cast simultaneously. The nozzles were controlled by stopper rods – steel rods sheathed with fireclay. By lifting a lever on the side of the ladle the rods could be raised and the metal would flow out. When ingot casting was completed the ladle would be turned upside down by the overhead crane, any slag remaining would then run out. The ladle lining would normally last up to twenty heats.

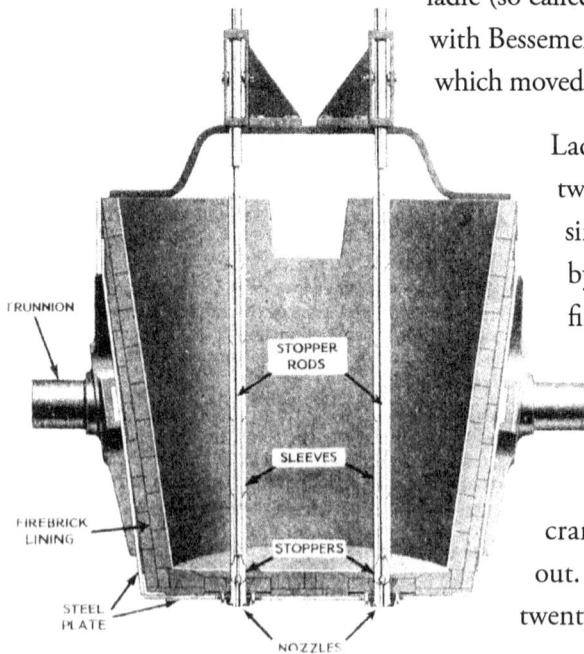

Cross-section of a Bessemer or bottom-pour ladle.
Courtesy of W. MacFarlane.

28

Steel ingots produced at Barrow varied in size over the years. The earliest made were in the region of 13 hundredweights, then 38 cwt. (nominally 2-tons), used for rolling down into rails. 5-ton ingots were for the heavy plate mill. (During the Second World War large 7-ton ingots were cast for processing elsewhere in the UK).

Immediately prior to the furnace being tapped one of the pitmen would set up a group of moulds in the casting pit. Ingot moulds were subject to severe conditions in service being constantly heated and cooled, and sometimes swung against a vertical stanchion when stripping proved difficult. On average mould life was around one hundred casts, it would then be scrapped. Sometime the newly teemed steel appeared 'wild' – as if boiling in the mould. A practice used at Barrow to induce quietness was called "stoppering the ingot". Sand was thrown on top of the steel followed by a heavy iron plate, on top of this a heavy weight was applied. When sufficient time had elapsed allowing the steel to cool and solidify the ingot was stripped from its mould. If insufficient time was allowed the ingot would 'bleed'. Serious accidents had happened in the past due to premature stripping.

The ingots were next clearly marked with their weight and cast number, also a cast card was generated by the clerk which would accompany the ingot through to the steel leaving the works, thereby ensuring full traceability.

Ingot casting from the 80-ton ladle, slag is cascading into tubs, note the suspended steel plate which is shielding the pit man and teemer from the intense heat. *Courtesy of Bill Myers.*

The mechanical ingot stripping plant, 1890s. Located towards the north-end of No.1 shed.
(This item of plant pre-dates the works plan on page 32, a battery of Babcock boilers occupying the original site).

The ingots were next loaded onto a railway wagon and shipped out of the shop.

Most of the ingots leaving the casting and stripping areas were transferred via the works internal rail network. (Apart from the addition of a few junctions and crossings this network changed very little in over a 100 years, it is recalled that during the 1970s roads were still known by the name they were given in the 1860s, i.e. plate mill road, Bessemer hill, slag road and so on).

Soaking pits were the invention of north east ironmaster John Gjers, they superseded the earlier reheating furnace of which, at one time, Barrow works had fifty-two. The advantages of the soaking pit were:- a) a saving of fuel, b) the ingot was handled and kept in a vertical

Another view of ingot casting from the 80-ton ladle, courtesy of F. Strike.

position, c) all sides of the ingot were heated evenly, and d) an increase in yield. The drawbacks were the awkwardness of the preliminary heating, the build-up of mill scale, and the uncertainty of maintaining a constant supply of hot ingots from the Siemens department.

At Barrow the soaking pits were fired on producer gas. They consisted of a series of fire-brick lined cells below the level of the steel shed floor. Deep archways of fire-brick supported the covers, and from these a large amount of heat was reflected.

The soaking pit crew standing in front of the pit covers, these covers were on wheels and were manoeuvred by the overhead crane facility. The chap in collar and tie is fuel technician Mr R. Walkden. 22nd February, 1956.

This kept the top part of the ingot particularly hot and thus prolonged the fluid and plastic conditions where most beneficial. The floor of the pits were of brick and silver sand. A myriad of culverts led from each section connecting to one main flue, this flue led to the famous big chimney (see photo on next page).

Departmental manager during the period under review was Bob Stokes known affectionately by his men as *Soakie Stokie*.

The northern end of No.2 steel shed, which housed the soaking pits and cogging mill, was provided with overhead cranage which comprised three overhead gantry cranes, from the north – was the Klondyke crane of 10-tons safe working load (swl), the Whip, a 5-ton swl fast crane used for feeding the cogging mill with ingots, and the south soaking pit crane another 10-ton swl Wellman used mainly for roll changing, some of which could be 8-tons in weight.

Part plan of the works showing, inter alia, the Siemens furnaces, blast furnaces, British Rail main line, soaking pits, Morgan gas producers and steel foundries, reproduced from BHS. Co. Plan 72.

Two views of the big chimney. Top is a 1951 shot taken from Walney Road. Courtesy of NW. Evening Mail. Below, a 1961 scene taken from the high-rise crane during the Barcon construction.

3

1942 and United Steel

By the start of the Second World War the works was both inefficient and dated. Despite the re-structuring of the 1920s most of the infrastructure was still very much Victorian.

The shock of Dunkirk in the spring of 1940, together with the blocking of Scandinavian special steels that were essential for munitions and ordnance manufacture, motivated Winston Churchill to concentrate alloy steel production at Barrow and Workington. (Both being on the furthest coast from the enemy).

In 1942 the steelworks and mills was requisitioned by the Ministry of Supply (MoS). The Haematite Steel Co had insufficient resources to bring the works into the 20th century. The United Steel Companies of Sheffield were appointed managing agent and the place became Ministry of Supply, Barrow Works. From 1948 the iron-smelting side became Barrow Ironworks Ltd.

United Steel's Piaggio G – APXK on the tarmac of Walney Aerodrome on 30th September 1965.

United Steel was formed in 1918 by the merging of shares of the UK's largest steel plants, later acquiring the Appleby Frodingham works at Scunthorpe also the Workington Iron and Steel Company. The United Steel combine were at the forefront of investment and innovation. Through heavy investment they had improved the efficiency of iron-smelting by the use of sintering. Steelmaking was improved by the development of the Ajax furnace (much to the credit of Albert Jackson, Ferro-metallurgist who later became a member of Barrow's Continuous Casting Steering Committee).

Upon taking over the running of Barrow works United Steel appointed their own man, Colonel G. N. F. Wingate, to works manager. Will Killingbeck accepted a role change focusing his attention on the now separate ironworks. Colonel Wingate was to oversee a phase of long overdue improvements. (From 1942 the ironworks was run as a separate business until its closure in 1963). Phase one entailed converting the larger furnaces from producer gas to oil and replacing the lever and chain mechanism on the furnace doors with hydraulic actuation. Part of the product rationalisation programme was the ceasing

The redoubtable Colonel Wingate, Steelworks Manager.

of rail production at Barrow and to concentrate such at Moss Bay steel plant at Workington – which had been under United Steel's control since 1919. Under United Steel Workington had been developed into one of the most modern steel plants in Europe. Barrow's core business, from 1942, would be making steel billets and slabs for re-rolling in its hoop and bar mills.

United Steel had invested heavily in improvements to the open hearth process at its Swinden Laboratories in Rotherham. Built after the Second World War, 240 specialised staff were employed in research and development. Barrow was about to benefit too from this research.

Fuelling with oil gives a hotter flame and thereby a faster rate of melting than with gas. The oil was injected into the furnace in the form of a fine spray after being atomised with a jet of steam. The burner and its atomiser were set into the furnace uptake as shown in the cross-sectional view on page 82 Oil burners worked under very hot conditions and required extensive water cooling; cooling water pipes were embedded into the furnace brickwork. Oil storage was by way of three large circular

The three large oil tanks photographed 2nd Feb 1961 during the construction of Barcon.
(Chimneys from No's 1, 2 and 3 furnaces are to the left of photo).

storage vessels sited to the south of the Siemens gantry, steam coils were fitted to each tank to raise the liquid fuel temperature to around 200°F. Additionally to provide further efficiency two new waste heat boilers were sited due north of the oil storage tanks, as the exhaust gases were in the region of 400°F. this was a very cost effective way of generating steam.

The aforementioned alterations had been completed by the end of the Second World War and improvement work now continued into peacetime. There had been talk of establishing a fuel and instrument department during the war but this was deferred until hostilities ended when personnel could be recruited from men leaving the armed forces.

One of the waste-heat boilers taken during demolition 2nd Feb 1961

The Fuel and Instrument Department was formed in 1946 and was the last phase of modernisations. It was set up so that instruments could be fitted to the furnaces and soaking pits to accurately record fuel flows, temperatures and pressures. It was deemed essential that daily records were kept so that

Staff of the Fuel and Instrument dept. in their original building. Back L to R: Bill Cousins, Gordon Jones, A. Payne and Ken Royall. Front L to R; J. Shepherd, Bert Jackson, C. Hooper, 24th May, 1954.

consumptions could be monitored and wastage kept to a minimum. The department, which was initially located on the first floor above the original Siemens laboratory, was also responsible for the design, construction, fitting and maintenance of all the thermocouples required for measuring the temperatures of the various processes. The accuracy of all the instruments was also checked daily and if found necessary, repair or re-calibration was undertaken in the departmental workshop. Bill Whiteside took over the fuel section of the department in 1955 when Chris Gunnee (a United Steel Man) returned to Sheffield. Ken Royall became overall department manager in 1959 when Whiteside transferred to continuous casting.

Ken Royall started at Barrow works in 1947 following demobilisation from the RAF where he had been a radio operator/air gunner. He started in the new department as an instrument technician and was assigned to fitting up the Siemens furnaces with instrument panels and temperature monitoring points. He reported that the difficult aspect of the task was not having to contend with the heat, dirt and potential danger but convincing the leading hands that the 'confounded instruments' were a much more accurate way of operating than their eye, ear and spit methods.

Ken Royall with fuel engineer Gordon Jones, 1966

Fuel technician Alec Finch with a furnace-metal pyrometer, 3rd Nov 1953.

A furnaceman (Walter Hubbold) taking the bath temperature of No.1 open hearth furnace – which was now fitted with the 'confounded instruments', 3rd Feb 1956.

Steelworks manager Mr T. G. Marple was the successor to Colonel Wingate in 1953. He had previously been Chief Engineer.

Ferro-metallurgist Mr A. J. Jackson was the main player with regard to United Steel's Ajax furnace project. He later joined the continuous casting steering committee at Barrow.

In February, 1951 the Labour government nationalised the main companies that made up the UK's iron and steel industry, a move which was strongly opposed by the opposition. So much so that on regaining power the Conservatives instructed the Corporation not to make any changes to the structure. After July, 1953 two new bodies were established with powers to operate, the Iron and Steel Holding and Realisation Agency, a temporary body to which was entrusted all the shares of iron and steel companies formerly owned by the Corporation, with a mandate to return the undertakings to private ownership; and the Iron and Steel Board, a permanent body with the authority to exercise public supervision over the industry. United Steel re-emerged in much the same form as its pre-nationalisation counterpart. (It would be another 14 years before the industry was again nationalised). Meanwhile in Barrow, not since the 1930s, hardship once again loomed as short-time working was introduced in the Siemens and mill departments.

An informal gathering of steel men at the Fisherman's Arms, Baycliff in 1964. Left to right are Mr Des Ainsbury, operations director, Mr Albert Jackson, Mr E. Aitkin, steelworks manager and Commander Wells of United Steel (Mr T. Marple's retirement) 30th June, 1964.

During the war years the works were producing quality steels which were being sent to munitions factories as well as supplying its own rolling mills. Now, the open hearth plant had a surplus capacity, more than could be processed up at the hoop mills. Most production departments went onto a 3 days per week rota.

It was also in the early 1950s that a glimmer of hope appeared on the horizon. An internal notice was posted , printed on Iron and Steel Board stationery, advising that Barrow had been designated an experimental works – no other details were given (the notice was obviously alluding to continuous casting research). The 85 years old steelworks was about to, once again, make the news.

(In 1961 the works was officially acquired by the United Steel Companies).

The company's limestone quarries at Stainton, near Dalton-in-Furness. The Crown and Devonshire quarries were a source of very pure carboniferous limestone. There was a kiln on-site providing a constant supply of lime, this was a staple of the basic steelmaking furnaces. From 1868 limestone had been transported from the quarry to Hindpool in wagons of the Furness Railway, in later years it was moved by road. *Courtesy of NW. Evening Mail.*

Photo taken to the south of the works, showing the extent of the rail network connecting the complex to the
Docks and Barrow Yard. The centre double tracks were the British Rail lines.
Michael Andrews, Geoff Holme collection (mac 48).

A south-bound passenger train, on its way into Barrow Central, passing the slag bank in 1954. This
predominant feature is the only tangible reminder of the works.
Michael Andrews, Geoff Holme collection.

4

The Siemens Laboratory

The original laboratory was situated on the west side of the Siemens scrap gantry near to the Morgan gas producers and can be seen by referring to the part plan of the works on page 32. Part of the post war modernisations included the building of a new lab and office block immediately south of the scrap gantry. The two storey building was of red engineering brick construction with metal window frames and a flat roof. The ground floor comprised store rooms and a mess room for the pit men and teemers. The first floor, accessed from two flights of stairs, included the chemistry lab, toilets and offices for management and clerical workers also a mess room for furnace workers. There was also a balcony to the rear, accessed from the first floor corridor, whereby managers could oversee the activity on the charging platform in the melting shop. The laboratory, provided with a clerestory roof (just visible in the photo below), had off-white tiling to three of the four walls. The chief chemist's office (Mr McDougal) and the balance room were at the west side with windows overlooking the main railway line and blast furnaces.

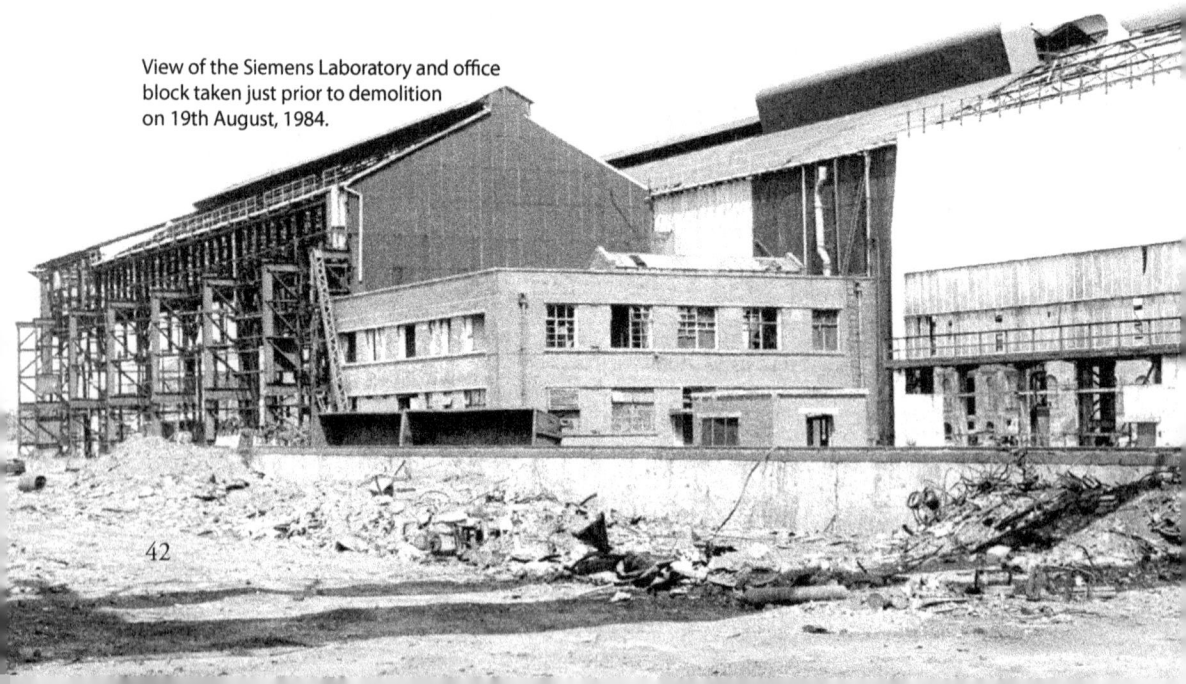

View of the Siemens Laboratory and office block taken just prior to demolition on 19th August, 1984.

Affixed to one of the tiled walls was the 'chemist's lament'. This is a parody on Kipling's famous poem IF, the identity of the wit responsible is lost in time, it was salvaged prior to demolition in 1984.

IF

(with apologies to Kipling)

If you can make the violent stinks invented, and work in them from morn till late at night,

Or with your lot be perfectly contented when you are asked to fool with dynamite;

If you can still remain quite calm and placid when plant officials effervesce and fret,

Or being told to test a fuming acid can suck it through an Icc pipette.

If you don't get just what the boss expected yet have the pluck the true results to state;

And never stoop to adding in the date, if you can read a bunch of sample numbers,

When all the labels have been soaked in crude, and can, when awakened from your slumbers,

At 2am respond in cheerful mood.

If you can drop the fruit of your exertion, before you've weighed it, on the concrete floor;

And feeling now a symptom of aversion, can start again as blithely as before;

If you can take a broken desiceator and from improvise a Liebig still,

Or gauge the rainfall by the dehydrator, and give three hours a week to first-aid drill.

If you can subjugate all thought of pleasure and still retain a meed of self-esteem,

If you can give your few short hours of leisure to keeping up with every modern theme;

If you donate your every waking minute, and seek your sole reward in duty done'

Yours is the Lab and all that's in it, and what is more you're welcome to it, Son.

The 'Chemist's Lament' (c/o Brian Cubbon)

On the north wall of the lab were three fume cupboards – one of which had a gas-fired hot plate- and these were used for the various analytical sampling processes (the hot plate was also convenient for heating eggs and bacon or pies), at one end of the cupboards was a fume extraction fan for expelling the toxic fumes generated.

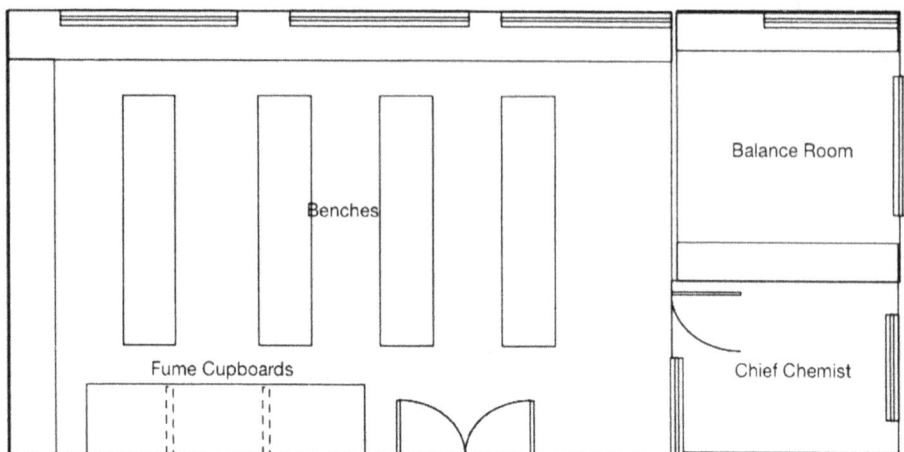

Sketch plan showing basic layout of the laboratory (nts). *Courtesy of Rodger Bradley.*

Throughout the 1950s and 60s the lab operated on a three-shift system. This was because every furnace heat had to have sample analysis. The shift pattern was – morning shift, 7am till 2pm; afternoon shift, 2pm till 9pm and night shift, 9pm until 7am.

Sartorius short beam analytical balance. Two balances were located in the room, the other being an Oertling chainomatic. *Courtesy of Brian Cubbon.*

Industrial chemist Bill Whiteside, Bill went from the lab to become head of the fuel section of the fuel and instrument department, moving later to continuous casting where he became one of the shift managers. Prior to works closure he was Barcon manager.

The senior chemists were Joe McMellin, and Dick Crellin. Junior chemists being Rodger Bradley, Frank Wignall, Walter Scott, John Miller, Vince Hall and David Anderson. Junior chemists worked in pairs i.e. two per shift.

5

Products

A study of the works and processes would not be complete without a discussion of the output from the works which, over the decades, was many and varied. The diagram below shows the breakdown across the three sections of the complex.

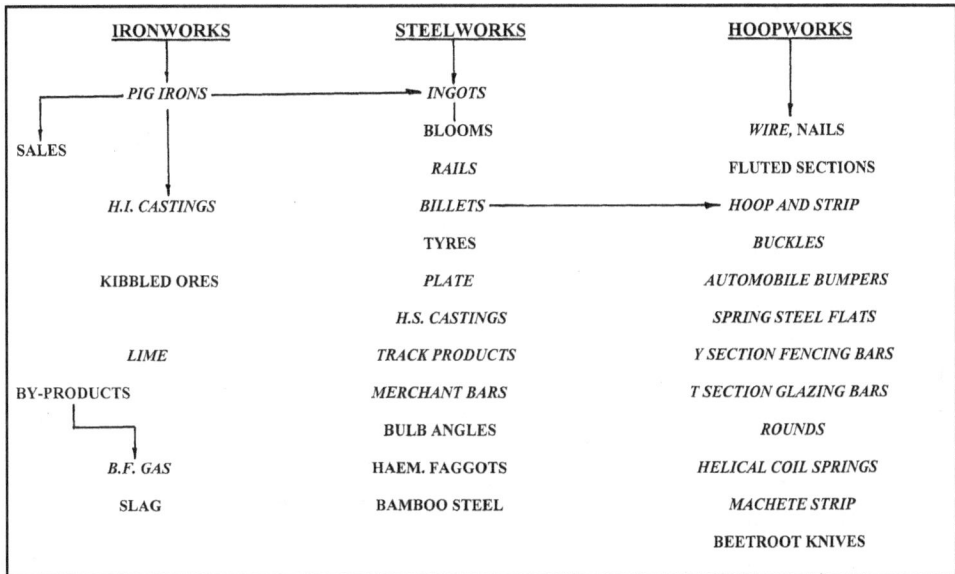

IRONWORKS	STEELWORKS	HOOPWORKS
PIG IRONS	INGOTS	
SALES	BLOOMS	WIRE, NAILS
	RAILS	FLUTED SECTIONS
H.I. CASTINGS	BILLETS	HOOP AND STRIP
	TYRES	BUCKLES
KIBBLED ORES	PLATE	AUTOMOBILE BUMPERS
	H.S. CASTINGS	SPRING STEEL FLATS
LIME	TRACK PRODUCTS	Y SECTION FENCING BARS
BY-PRODUCTS	MERCHANT BARS	T SECTION GLAZING BARS
	BULB ANGLES	ROUNDS
B.F. GAS	HAEM. FAGGOTS	HELICAL COIL SPRINGS
SLAG	BAMBOO STEEL	MACHETE STRIP
		BEETROOT KNIVES

Diagram of the output across the three sections of the works. *S. Henderson*

Prior to the formation of the Barrow Haematite Steel Company the main product had been pig iron. During 1862 – 63 over 120,000 tons was sent to more industrial areas in the country, such as Yorkshire and South Wales. Pig iron continued to be exported from the town but in addition, from 1865, a large proportion was directed to the new Bessemer plant and then for about six months, until the new rolling mills came on line, haematite steel ingots of 2, and 5-tons were made and sold.

By 1869 the new mills were producing over 1000-tons of rails per week and also tyre ingots for locomotive wheels. At the time of writing nothing is known of the tyre mills. Locomotive wheels are expensive to produce and so fitting a replaceable wearing element, such as a steel tyre, is a way of preserving the wheel casting. The tyre would be machined at a locomotive works (such as the workshop of the Furness Railway Company at Rabbit Hill, Barrow), to have an 'interference fit' with the wheel, it would next be heated sufficiently and while in an expanded state would be attached to the wheel. Upon cooling it would be a tight, secure fit. The following photo is of a tyre mill working at Horwich railway works in 1919. It is to be assumed that, apart from being powered by a vertical engine, the Barrow mill was not entirely dissimilar.

From 1874 mild steel plate was produced for shipbuilding. Steel was becoming the preferred material for hull construction and was slowly replacing iron. Sizes rolled were 0.25 inch up to 1.5 inch in thickness. Steel plate was available in widths as rolled (7 feet 6 inches) and in random lengths. Bulb-angles were also made. These were a shipbuilding section and were used as stiffeners and for the ribs of a ship's hull, being secured to the plates with rivets. After rolling, plate was cooled then made available for inspection by agents of the classification societies, Admiralty and Board of Trade surveyors.

A tyre rolling mill, 1919. (Driven by a vertical steam engine) *Courtesy of National Rail Museum and SSPL.*

Survey of products from the Open Hearth Years.

Pig Iron: Also referred to at Barrow as bar-iron, was consistently made and sold on until 1963. Haematite pig iron was produced from selected haematite ores and first-class cokes, thereby ensuring a minimum of impurities. Pig iron was sold to guaranteed analysis. Blast furnace iron was supplied in sand cast pigs measuring 4" x 4" x 18"/24" and with normal proportion of sows unless otherwise specified by customers. Pig iron could also be supplied in medium sized pigs, 3" x 3" x 18" or small pigs, 2" x 2" x 12". In blast furnace haematite the total carbon content remained constant at 3.75 to 4.25 per cent. In refined pig irons, tolerances could be reduced and a wider range is possible in all elements.

Semi-phosphoric Foundry Pig Iron: Barrow semi phosphoric pig iron (brand s.p.) was an 'all-mine' iron designed after extensive investigations into defects most common to iron castings. Used for such as cylinders and valves etc. it was of outstanding quality.

Ingots: Supplied in acid or basic and manufactured by the Siemens Martin Open Hearth Process.

Tyre Ingots: Including hexagonal, supplied to all specifications.

Blooms: In acid, basic or alloy, for re-rolling or forging etc. sizes made:-
from 51/2 up to 8" square also 6"x 5" and 8" x 6", finished with radius corners.

Slabs: 4"x11/4", 4"x 11/2", 5"x 11/4", 4"x 11/2", 5"x 11/2", 4"x 2", 5"x 2", 6"x 2", 7"x 2", 71/2"x 2", 8"x 2" and 9"x 2". All with radius corners.

Steel Rails:
All British standard sections, both flat-bottomed and bull-head. Old or revised sections also A.S.C.E. sections. From 10lbs to 120lbs per yard. (Rolls could be cut for special sections).

Flat-bottom (*Vignole*) rails in marshalling area awaiting despatch. *Courtesy of Richard Byers.*

THE LABORATORY.

Barrow Hæmatite Steel Company, Limited.

June 8th., 19.43.

SIEMEN'S BASIC ACID STEEL. London, Midland & Scottish Rly. 95lbs. B.H.Rails.

Percentage of Carbon & Phosphorus in Drillings from following Casts :

x 2500/5/36

Cast	Carbon	Phos.	Cast	Carbon	Phos.	Cast	Carbon	Phos.	Cast	Carbon	Phos.
970	.56	.040	980	.55	.042	2250	.53	.035	-	-	-

THE LABORATORY.

Barrow Hæmatite Steel Company, Limited.

June 15th., 19.43.

SIEMEN'S BASIC ACID STEEL.   London, Midland & Scottish Rly.   95lbs.B.H.Rails.

Percentage of Carbon & Phosphorus in Drillings from following Casts :

x 2500/5/36

Cast	Carbon	Phos.	Cast	Carbon	Phos.	Cast	Carbon	Phos.	Cast	Carbon	Phos.
974	.55	.056	985	.59	.034	1009	.50	.023	2283	.55	.034

49

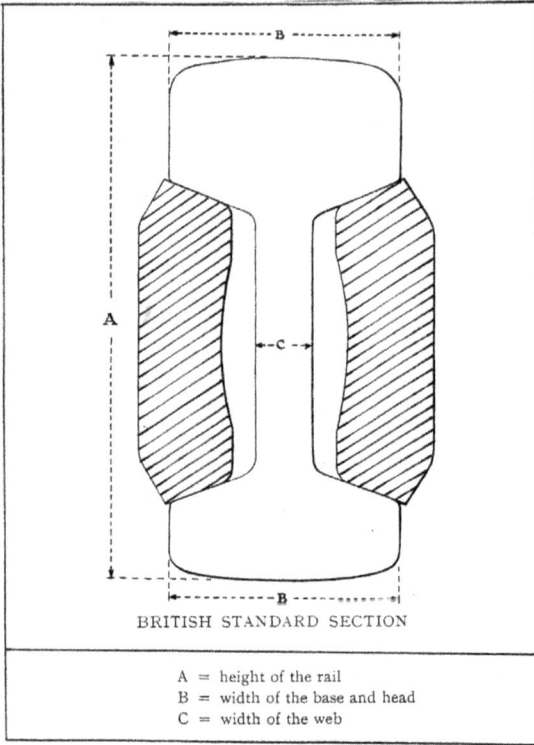

BRITISH STANDARD SECTION

A = height of the rail
B = width of the base and head
C = width of the web

section of Bull-Head rail with fishplates.

FLAT-BOTTOM RAIL
WITH SHALLOW AND ANGLE FISHPLATES

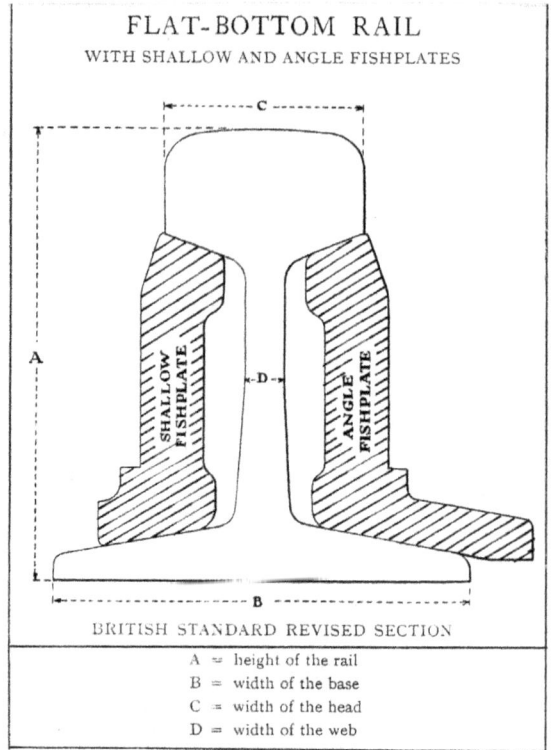

SHALLOW FISHPLATE

ANGLE FISHPLATE

BRITISH STANDARD REVISED SECTION

A = height of the rail
B = width of the base
C = width of the head
D = width of the web

Section of Flat-Bottom rail with, left, shallow
fishplate and right, angle fishplate.

COLLIERY RAILS

TYPICAL SECTION OF COLLIERY BRIDGE RAIL

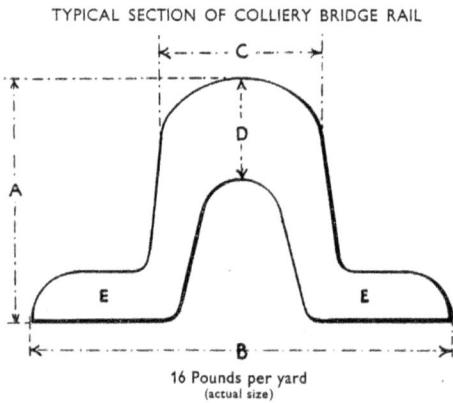

16 Pounds per yard
(actual size)

A = height of the rail.   C = width of the head.
B = width of the base.   D = depth of the head.
          E = thickness of the flange.

LIGHT BRIDGE RAILS, BRITISH STANDARD MINES
SECTIONS

COLLIERY RAILS

TYPICAL SECTION OF
FLAT-BOTTOM COLLIERY RAIL

A = height of the rail. B = width of the base.
C = width of the head. D = width of the web.

British Standard Light Flat-bottom Rail
for use in Mines.

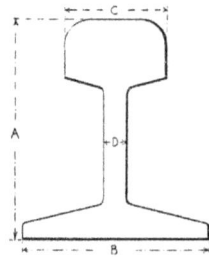

25 lbs. per yard

LIGHT FLAT-BOTTOM RAILS AND FISHPLATES

British Standard Mines Sections (Conforming to B.S.
Specification No. 248-1926)

50

FAGGOT SQUARES AND FAGGOT FLATS

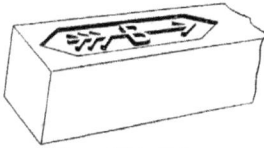

From $\frac{1}{2}''$ to $1\frac{1}{2}''$ sq.

From $1'' \times \frac{1}{4}''$ to $3'' \times \frac{3}{8}''$

MILANO SQUARE STEEL

Hardened or unhardened as required
In bundles, boxes or kegs for export

BAMBOO STEEL

$\frac{3}{8}''$, $\frac{1}{2}''$, $\frac{5}{8}''$, $\frac{3}{4}''$, $\frac{7}{8}''$, $1''$, $1\frac{1}{4}''$ and $1\frac{1}{2}''$

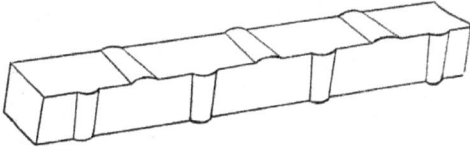

MATCHETT STEEL

1, 2 or 3 Groove

$1\frac{3}{4}'' \times$ 10 gauge to 14 gauge up to $2\frac{1}{2}'' \times$ 9 gauge to 13 gauge

BEVELS

Beetroot Knife

55 and 50 m/m. x 8 m/m. x 2 m/m.
$\frac{7}{8}'' \times 1\frac{1}{16}'' \times 1\frac{3}{16}''$ to $\frac{5}{8}'' \times \frac{7}{16}'' \times \frac{5}{16}''$
$1\frac{3}{4}'' \times 1\frac{3}{8}'' \times 1\frac{1}{4}''$

FILE STEEL

Square, 3-Square, Flat, Round or Half-Round in all
Standard sizes

FLUTED SECTIONS

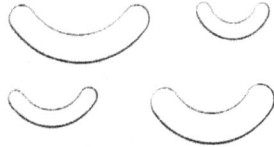

For Bucket and Kettle Handles, etc., in all standard sizes

AUTOMOBILE BUMPER BARS
Supplied in spring steel to customers' specifications.

CORRUGATED $3\frac{1}{2}'' \times \frac{1}{4}''$

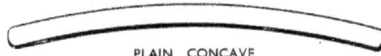

CORRUGATED $3'' \times \frac{1}{4}''$

PLAIN CONCAVE
$3\frac{1}{2}'' \times \frac{1}{4}''$ to $2'' \times \frac{3}{16}''$

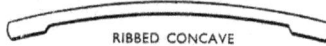

RIBBED CONCAVE
$3'' \times \frac{3}{8}'' \times \frac{3}{16}''$
$2\frac{1}{2}'' \times \frac{3}{16}'' \times \frac{3}{32}''$

RIBBED CONCAVE $2\frac{1}{2}'' \times \frac{3}{16}'' \times \frac{1}{4}''$

PLAIN "D" SECTION
$1\frac{3}{4}'' \times \frac{23}{32}''$

FLUTED "D" SECTION
$1\frac{1}{2}'' \times \frac{9}{16}''$

$1\frac{3}{4}'' \times \frac{1}{4}'' \times \frac{11}{16}''$

$1\frac{1}{2}'' \times \frac{3}{16}'' \times \frac{11}{16}''$

$1\frac{3}{4}'' \times \frac{1}{4}'' \times \frac{7}{16}''$
GROOVED SECTIONS

51

Also provided were chrome steel for tracks subject to heavy traffic. Conductivity rails and copper bearing and manganese – to approved specifications.

Fishplates: Both shallow and angle sections.

Soleplates: Also special track fittings to suit all sections of rails.

Bamboo Steel: This was produced for civil engineering applications eg: Re-enforcing bars.

Haematite Steel Castings: Used in areas subject to high stresses where haematite iron was not suitable. See chapter one, page 14, for typical example.

Hoop and Strip: the largest section was produced by No.3 mill. Hoop issuing from the finishing rolls was directed towards the vertical coiling machinery. Where customers did not require their hoop coiled, Barrow works had a machine called a *cold-reeler*. This machine comprised a turntable at one end where a coil of hoop would be placed, the end of the hoop would be fed into a train of rolls and these straightened out the hoop as it passed through, being sheared into six-foot lengths. These lengths dropped into a trough where labourers would count and carry them off in bundles to the bundling table. Cold reeling was a labour intensive process.

A smaller section was produced on No.2 mill. Known as 'strip', this was in the order of 0.03in thick used for cable tape and cotton tie. Strip issuing from No.2 mill finisher, unlike No.3, was discharged along a compressed-air cooled channel 250 feet long. 0.03-in. is the thinnest that steel can be rolled-down to. It can be stated here that the mills at Barrow were the first to roll steel hoop, offering them for sale in 1872, and they were considered unsurpassed for ductility and uniformity of temper.

Bundles of coiled hoop awaiting shipment. These were products of No.3 Hoop Mill, after rolling the hoop was coiled on the vertical coiling machinery.

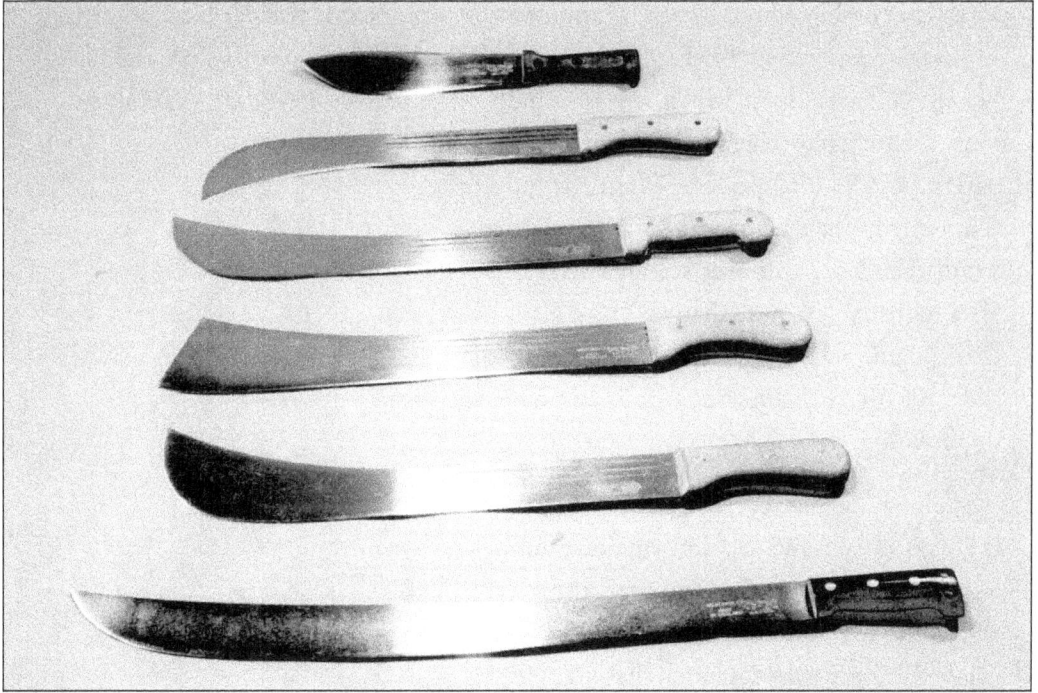

Various types of machete made from Barrow steel.
These were rolled on the double duo, A-side and finished at the works of Ralph Martindale and Company.

SPRING STEEL

SQUARE BEVELS

$\frac{1}{2}$" to $1\frac{1}{8}$" rising by $\frac{1}{16}$" with $\frac{1}{16}$"
Bevel each side.

$1\frac{3}{16}$" to 1" rising by $\frac{1}{16}$". 1" to $2\frac{3}{4}$"
rising by $\frac{1}{8}$" with $\frac{1}{8}$" Bevel each
side.

BEVEL SPRING BARS

for the manufacture of Helical Springs (round or square edges)

Width   — — — $\frac{5}{8}$" to $2\frac{1}{2}$"
Thickness   — — — $\frac{1}{4}$" to $1\frac{1}{4}$"
            at any intervals

NOTE.—Dimensions of Bevels
should be stated as $A \times B \times C$.

Examples of spring steel sections, rolled on No.1 mill.

Having completed our excursion through the open hearth years at Barrow works, all that remains is for a brief summing-up. It is now over thirty years since the town lost the industry upon which it was founded. The British Steel Corporation, who took a hatchet to the works, as well as many others, has also disappeared. Where the industry is heading in the 21st century is anyone's guess. I don't think we will ever see another British Steel Industry any more than we will a National Coal Board. Such things are now firmly in the hands of overseas concerns – as is commercial shipbuilding.

Steelmaking has come a long way since the days of spit-and-see and rule-of-thumb. Skills developed at Barrow over the years, acknowledged and revered around the world, where a furnace man could tell that his 'fire' was at tapping temperature simply by looking at it or assess the carbon content of a sample by the

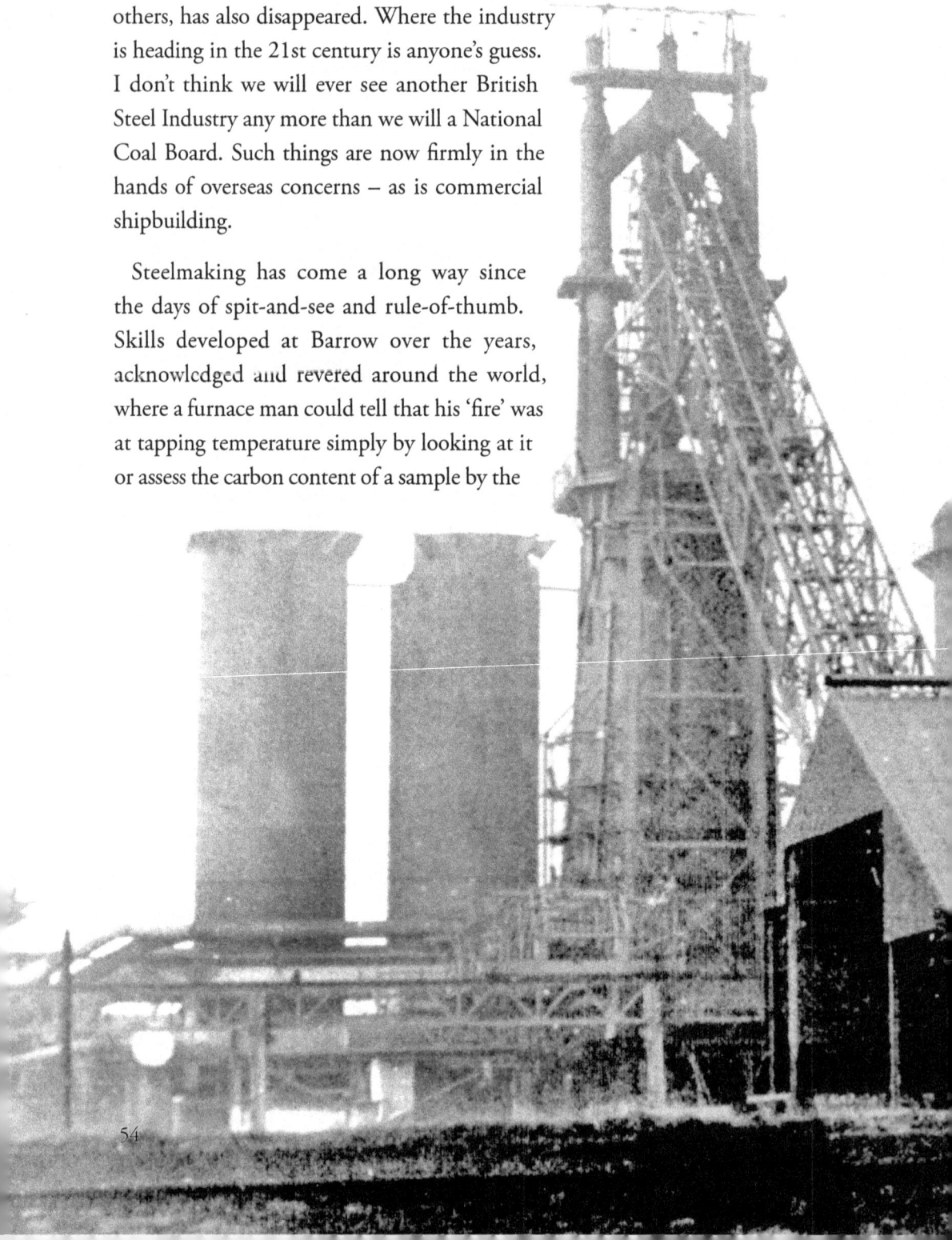

appearance of its fracture when broken, are now achieved through technology in processes not available to the early ironmasters. Some works have survived by moving into the 'specialist' area, working in complicated alloys which are only needed in small quantities and made in an induction furnace. Barrow was on the brink of moving into this area, had it still have been under United Steel control many believe it would have. These complicated alloys which include some of the 'newer' materials like titanium for instance, cannot be refined in the furnace and have to be melted in vacuum conditions. They are not really steel in that they no longer retain the defining property of magnetism, nevertheless they are made by steelmakers. And there the matter must rest.

Good God, is that the time . . .?

View looking west from the Siemens Laboratory. No 2 blast furnace is on the left, this made the semi-phosphoric (s.p.) pig iron referred to earlier in this chapter. Four in number hot blast stoves stand between No's 2 and 3 furnaces. (No 3 was the new furnace, it had a potential capacity of 4,000-tons per week). To the right, but not in the frame, is No 4 furnace this was normally kept on a haematite charge. The charging system, via the inclines, worked on the Pohlig pattern. Courtesy of R. Walkden 1964.

Appendix 1

Some More Key Personnel Over the Years

(Continued from the 2015 volume)

William Killingbeck
General Manager, later Chairman and Managing Director of Barrow Ironworks

J. K. Howarth	Managing Director, Barrow Iron works Ltd (successor to the above)
J. Williamson	Company Secretary Barrow Ironworks Ltd
G. Metcalfe	Company Secretary. Steelworks
E. A. Aitkin	Steelworks Manager
T. R. Maguire	Assistant Manager Siemens Dept., later Barcon Manager
K. Law	Central Works Department, later Planning Manager
W. Whiteside	Industrial Chemist, later a Barcon Manager
W. Caldwell	Shift Manager Continuous Casting
Wilf Bradshaw	Manager, New Bank and Bright Bar
Don Cottam	Electrical Manager, acting Works Manager prior to closure.
'Sheffield' Sam Newbold	Roof Maintenance/Steeplejacks
Bill Bright	Ganger
J. Rogan	Blast furnace manager
A. Repton	Foreman Plumber, Gas & Water Department
G. McCauley	Foreman Plumber, Gas & Water Department
H. Grainger	Foreman Bricklayer, Building Department
Dollar Smith	Roller, No.2 Rail Mill
D. Metcalfe	Building Department Manager

R. Metcalfe	Stores and Personnel
J. McDougal	Chief Chemist, Siemens Laboratory
Leo Woods	Metallurgy Laboratory
Des Campbell	Research Laboratory
Henry Thompson	Research Laboratory, manager
H. Barnes	Roller, No.1 Bar Mill.
Harold Baines,	Roller, No.2 Hoop Mill
Cliff Hunt	Roller, No.3 Hoop Mill
Bill Shepherd	Roller, No.3 Hoop Mill
Harry Wharman	Roller, No.3 Hoop Mill
Bill Walker	Roller, Double Duo, A-Side
John Dixon	Roller, Double Duo, B-Side
Sister Beattie	Ambulance Room/Clinic

Other Agencies

Company Solicitors	Messrs Hart Jackson
Shipping Agents	James Fisher and Sons. Ltd.
Road Transport	T.Brady & Son, Transport and Warehousing
Bankers	National Provincial Bank.

Appendix 2

The Board of Directors, 1899 (and into the 1900s)

His Grace the 8th Duke of Devonshire.

Mr Victor C. W. Cavendish, MP

Sir Henry M. Meysey-Thompson, Bart., MP *

Sir David Dale, Bart. *

Mr W. A. Donaldson. *

Mr John Fell

Mr W. F. Egerton

Mr W. M. F. Schneider.

Company Secretary: Mr A. Butchart.

His Grace, the 8th Duke of Devonshire.
(The absent Chairman). *Courtesy of NWE Mail*

The Chairman of the Barrow Haematite Steel Company during the period under review was Spencer Compton Cavendish, 8th Duke of Devonshire, who had succeeded his father in that capacity twelve years previously. The Duke spent little time in Barrow. Victor C. W. Cavendish was heir-presumptive to the Dukedom of Devonshire. Henry M. Meysey-Thompson (Lord Knaresborough) was a well-known railway and agricultural authority in the north of England and a director of the North-Eastern Railway. David Dale was a managing partner in the great coke and iron ore producing firm of Pease and Partners, Darlington, and also a director of North-eastern Railway. (Henry Pease would go on to be the founder of modern Middlesbrough). W. A. Donaldson was a principal of the distinguished Scottish and Middlesbrough firm of James Watson and Company. John Fell, ironmaster, had long been connected with the fortunes of the Furness district. W. F. Egerton was a member of the Devonshire family (son-in-law of the 7th Duke). Frank Schneider whose father, along with his partner Robert Hannay, started the first blast furnaces at Hindpool which led to the evolution of the entire complex.

* The east-coast interests in the Company were now obvious.

(Reference to the Board was made in an issue of *Punch*, viz . . With two Dukes amongst its directors, to say nothing of Lord knows who, in the way of Lords, and Lord knows how many millionaires! . .)

A great loss on the local scene was the sudden unexpected death, during the open hearth years, of William Killingbeck, Chairman and managing director of Barrow Ironworks Ltd. Killingbeck had been the last general manager of the Hindpool works right up to the 1942 split when the steel making side was hived off by the Government.

Mr Killingbeck died suddenly in London in March, 1959 eight months before the works celebrated its centenary. He joined the company just after the First World War and worked his way to the top becoming a much respected leader. Although not a Barrovian it was said he had the interests of the town and the local iron and steel industry at heart.

His funeral was attended by leaders of all the district's industries, financial institutions and professional people. Leonard Redshaw, director and general manager of Vickers-Armstrong Shipbuilders, said "During Mr Killingbeck's long association with the iron and steel industry there have been many fluctuations and crises but, to his credit, he steered his company successfully through many difficult periods, retaining at all times his ambition to maintain in this district an active and successful heavy industry running parallel with Vickers Armstrong. . ."

Thomas Marple, general manager of Barrow Steelworks, said "Mr W. Killingbeck was the complete personification of the English gentleman, kind to his employees, loving to his family and generous to his friends. Energy and power radiated from his whole being, and although he could be firm and resolute in business, he could be magnanimous and kindly to all who sought his aid. . ."

William Killingbeck was eventually superseded at the works by James Kenneth Howarth, a Holker Old Boy, who had started at the works as a youth.

From 1942 the steelmaking side of the works was hived off by the Government and ran as Ministry of Supply, Barrow Works. From 1948 the blast furnace departments became Barrow Ironworks Ltd. Following nationalisation and subsequent de-nationalisation (1951/52) of the industry – which brought an untimely death to many independent companies – it was enterprisingly split up into several concerns, still controlled from its head office at Priors Lea, Barrow. These concerns comprised: -

Pennington ore mill, Stainton quarries, a foundry division and the Darwen and Mostyn Iron Company, Flintshire, North Wales. This boasted a modern blast furnace and was the only independent producer of Ferro-manganese and Spiegelsein *(Employing about 350).

(By 1932 the Company had sold the colliery, coke ovens and by-products plant at Worsboro', south Yorkshire, to Barrow Barnsley Main Collieries Ltd.)

• These two alloys were called finishing materials because they were important final additions to the steelmaking process.

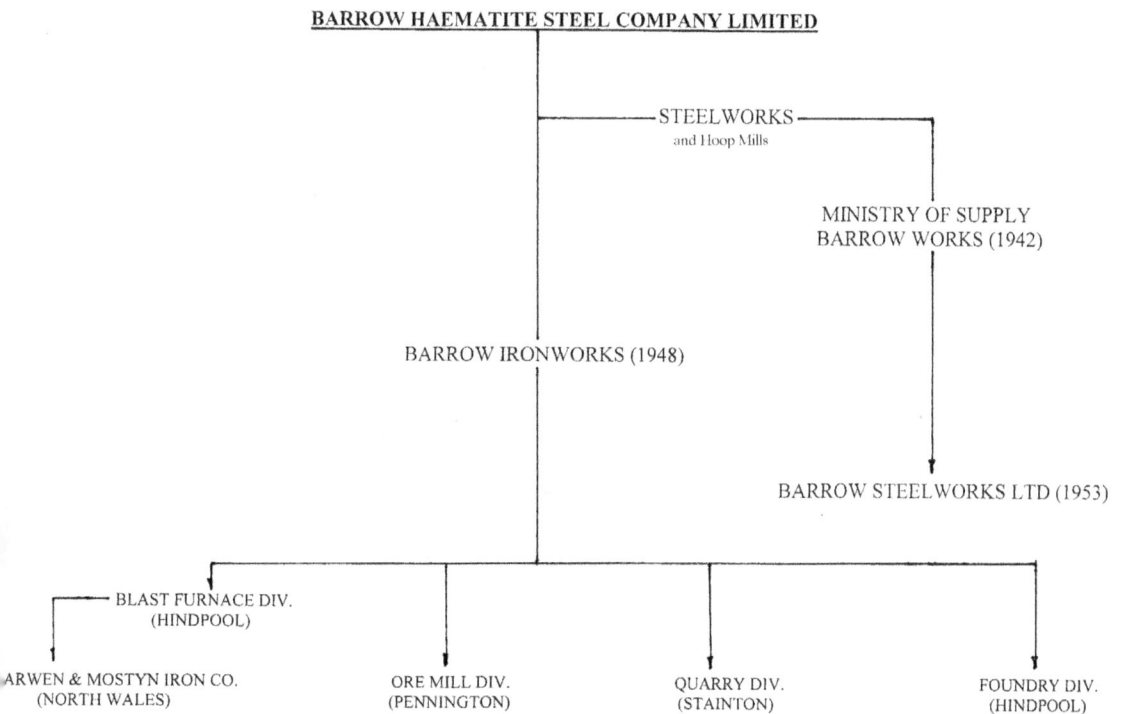

BARROW HAEMATITE STEEL COMPANY LIMITED

STEELWORKS
and Hoop Mills

MINISTRY OF SUPPLY
BARROW WORKS (1942)

BARROW IRONWORKS (1948)

BARROW STEELWORKS LTD (1953)

BLAST FURNACE DIV.
(HINDPOOL)

ARWEN & MOSTYN IRON CO.
(NORTH WALES)

ORE MILL DIV.
(PENNINGTON)

QUARRY DIV.
(STAINTON)

FOUNDRY DIV.
(HINDPOOL)

Splitting of the Barrow Haematite Steel Company from 1942. (Diagram). S. Henderson

Siemens Laboratory (Ref. Chapter 4)

Senior chemist, Dick Crellin was a character. It is recalled that on occasion he would play a practical joke on some unsuspecting junior chemist. He would prepare gun cotton – basically cotton wool soaked in sulphuric acid and then carefully dried. When unsuspecting prey walked by, Dick would place a piece on their shoulder setting fire to it. The result was most spectacular with an ear warming effect, the look of horror on the sap's face evoked uncontrolled laughter throughout the lab. Rodger Bradley, shift chemist.

Building Department.

The building department was the largest department on the works. Dick Metcalf (no relation to the brothers Geoff and Ronny) was the manager, and was a quite senior man in the management hierarchy (post WW2). Brickie Edwin Whitehead, whose foreman was Harold Grainger, recalled the work involved in re-lining a furnace. "Every so often the furnaces had to have their fire-brick linings renewed. This would be several times per year including stop fortnight (the works summer shut-down). Following a last heat on a Friday night – say about 9pm – the furnace working doors would be fully opened and large electric fans positioned to blow cooling air into the vessel. Such was the accumulation of heat that at 6am the next morning a man could enter the furnace for no longer than about twenty seconds. Then as the furnace cooled men would start to go in with crow bars to break up the slag skull and start removing the old brickwork and debris. This was a very dirty, hot and strenuous task requiring several shifts of men who would work in rotation – perhaps one hour about". Upon removal of all the debris an inspection of the furnace internal structure would take place after which the brickies would begin the re-lining process. In the case of an acid furnace the hearth would be lined with silica bricks and sand. With a basic furnace, magnesite and chrome magnesite bricks, together with rammed dolomite, would be used. When the re-lining was completed it was absolutely imperative the 'mortar' was allowed to dry out before the furnace was put back into service. Sometimes small wood fires were set to hasten the drying process.

"The art of the steelmaker is to vary the chemical composition and physical properties of the finished metal in such a way that it meets the exacting requirements of the customer" Joe Lyon, chief metallurgist, Barrow works, talking about matchet steel in 1965.

Brickies at work re-lining an 80-ton capacity Bessemer steel ladle.

Talking about matchet steel. . .pictured above are Mr R. C. Moore and Mr R. R Ralph of Ralph Martindale and Company after their visit to Barrow on 30th September, 1965. Martindale was the firm that turned matchet steel into machete and other quality handtools. Seeing them off is commercial manager E. G. Kite, right.

Joe Lyon (his family owned Lyon's chemist in Hartington St, Barrow) chain-smoked Capstan full strength cigarettes. During a conversation with his nephew Derek Lyon (Barrow's town clerk at the time of the works closure) in 2014, Mr Lyon told me that his uncle never offered a cigarette to anyone and that he could peel an orange in his pocket. I therefore claim the distinction of being the only person to whom he offered a cigarette. Stan Henderson jnr.

Mr J. Lyon, MBE, chief metallurgist during the United Steel years. Photo taken 23rd May 1964

Appendix 3

Bill Pearson (Uncle Willy) started at the works in 1913 age14 years as a Blower's assistant on the Bessemers. From there he went into the Siemens department where he stayed until 1951, after this date he moved to the continuous casting pilot plant as leading hand on the arc furnace. Bill was the works most experienced and senior furnaceman, he was held in high regard by local management.

The avuncular Bill Pearson, 1963.

Throughout the 1950s and 60s Bill was known affectionately as Uncle Willy by the children of Hood Street, Hindpool. During the summer months he would often sit on his back-door step and amuse the children playing in the back street and would regale us with stories about the steelworks and things he had seen. He would also dole out sweets on a regular basis, needless to say he was very popular. Bill retired in 1963, on the day he finished he was taken to the manager's office for tea and biscuits. A send-off not usually extended to blue collar workers in those days.

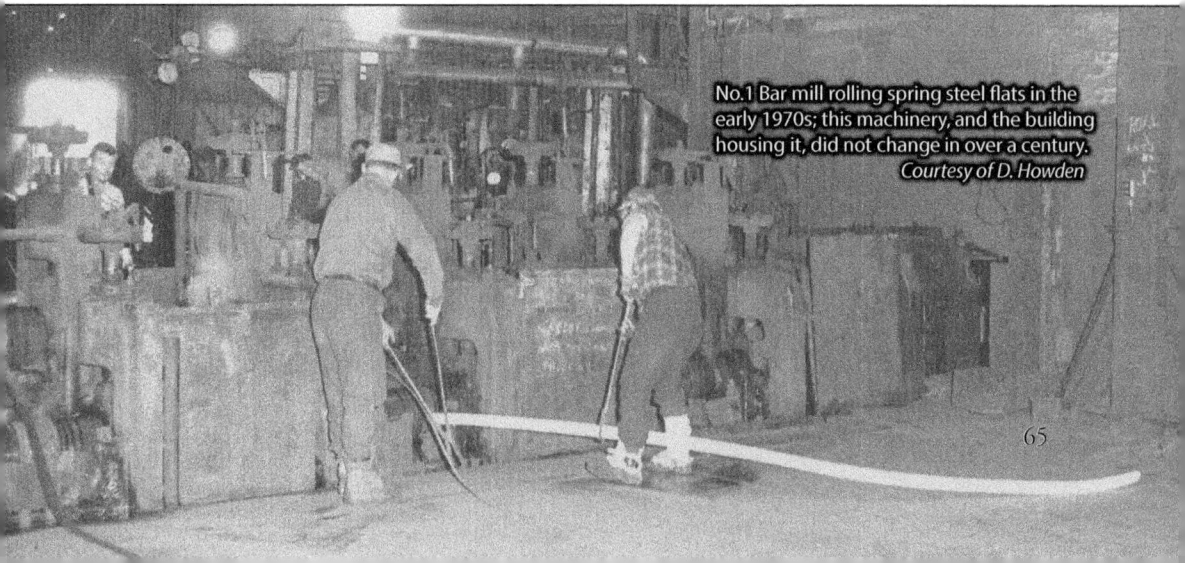

No.1 Bar mill rolling spring steel flats in the early 1970s; this machinery, and the building housing it, did not change in over a century.
Courtesy of D. Howden

Hindpool Hotel – long closed – is at the left of the terrace on Hindpool Road. For many years it was the regular haunt of iron workers, it was said to have the longest bar in the town. At the other end of the terrace, but not in the frame, was the Wheatsheaf. In 1873 only the two pubs stood on that stretch of the road, the houses in-between were built several years later. The photo was taken from the north corner of Gradwell's yard during the construction of Athersmith's garage. *Courtesy of T. Brady and son Ltd.*

Following his retirement Bill was a mine of information regarding the early years of the works; but you could always tell when you had taken-up too much of his time, he would look at his watch and say, "good God is that the time? 10 o'clock and not a pot washed!"

My father started in the merchant mill from school in 1939 (mentored by mill boss Fred Parry), at the time it was rolling fish plates and point rodding. He was laid-off six months later when the mill closed down and the works ceased production of track products. Throughout the war he worked on Walney farms and then in 1946 worked on the bolting rolls of No.3 mill at the hoop works. In those days he had to have three sweat-shirts when he went on shift, one he would wear to work and two in his haversack. He said that after the first hour he needed to put on a dry shirt. The job he did was so hot and strenuous that he was allowed to rest for 20 minutes in every hour (during the summer months barley water was provided free issue). In the last hour of his shift his last shirt would be bone-dry – he said there was no sweat left in his body to come out. He left the hoop works in 1951, he always maintained the place was a hell-hole. He came back again in 1956 crane driving on the Siemens pit and then in 1958 he joined the experimental team on the pilot plant moving latterly onto Barcon. He would always say that no-one should have to work like the men of No.3 mill.

S. Henderson

My dad Malcolm McPoland used to work in the No.1 mill, in fact he was there until it closed down. Because of the heat he had absolutely no hair on the front of his body, he nevertheless said it was a happy place to work. Carol McPoland

"Remember when we were about 10-years old (1959) Stan and we would be playing on the swings at Piggy Lane with David and Keith Reynolds of Hood Street, we thought that the steelworks' offices were Hindpool town hall." Bob Brady of T. Brady transport and warehousing talking to Stan Henderson, August, 2015.

My first day at Barrow Works

As I walked along Duke Street at noon on that first day my attention was seized by the big chimney – the tallest one on the site, on a clear day it was visible from the summit of Coniston Old Man. Some of the men were coming off-shift and heading for the public house – the Queens Hotel. I continued on towards 'Hindpool town hall'. Crossing Walney Road I took the workman's entrance into the clocking station where I was accosted by the gate man, a cripple known only to me as Billy K-legs, who directed me to one of the time-keepers. The clocking station was tranquil and scrupulously clean, as were all the offices I had occasion to enter. I was struck by an unusual, but not unpleasant smell and one I had not encountered before or since. No vending machines or cheap plastic cups here, this was the home of Quality; the place could have been the setting for a H. G. Wells story. The only sound pervading the silence was the movement of the time pieces. (These were wound twenty-eight times once per week by the timekeepers). I was given a time card and told to memorise my clock number, then directed to the Test House.

Looking west along Hindpool Road, the Wheatsheaf is on the right with the Barcon in the distance. This pub at one time was arguably the town's most popular destination, drinkers would queue to imbibe its quality beers and ribald humour. Early 1970s.
Courtesy of D. Gardiner.

The New Inn formerly the Hammer and Pincers, stood at the corner of Franklin Street and Steel Street in lower Hindpool. Built in 1861 by local contractor William Gradwell, it used to supply 'near beer' which was taken into the works in white enamel jugs by wives and mothers. *Photo by kind permission of NWE Mail.*

The Test House was only a short distance from the main entrance being located next to the time office. Inside I was greeted by foreman Bill Roderick who I knew from Dundonald Street, Hindpool, he took me for a brief introduction to the boss, Mr Lyon, chief metallurgist and a man of few words. Bill Roderick, as well as being test house foreman, was in charge of independent inspection. In a nutshell this was quality control but before it became a religion. I was next put in the care of utility man Roly Hill a genial character who wore a black beret and smoked incessantly, a pastime, it seemed, of everyone in the department. (Roly was one of several employees used as a 'knocker-up'. When someone was needed in work say, through the night, because of accident or illness – or in the case of a derailment - when our neighbour Joe Baker, boss platelayer, was called out, the knocker-up swung into action). An introduction to the micrometer cupboard was first on the induction agenda where a full set of Moore and Wright were kept. I was told how they were precision instruments not to be abused (apparently my predecessor had tried using the 0 to 1 as an adjustable spanner!). It was part of my role to manage the loaning-out of these instruments. My job appeared to be a doddle until . . . later in the day I was shown 'my' wheelbarrow, this was a huge metal cart with two large cast iron wheels. I was to push this? I was next sent across the works to collect a set of chain slings and bring them back for heat treatment and testing. I firmly believed that had the RSPCA seen this vehicle, they would have forbade its use in connection with any beast of burden. Entering No.1 steel shed I witnessed the death of the sun. The interior of this 'cathedral' put me in mind of St Pancras railway station. There was a perplexity of iron lying about in eccentric and perverse forms. I began to feel the throb of Barcon. Red hot, white hot steel; fireworks showering from under the casting machines – an iron taste, an iron smell and a confusion of iron sounds. This was a place to make a man's headache, but it was also very much a man's domain. I was awestruck.

At 4pm and very nearly at the end of my first day (finishing time was 4.06pm) I was again approached by Mr Roderick, he asked if I would mind working Sunday as one of the examiners, Arthur Hampshire – a spark tester – had gone into hospital with a perforated ulcer. I agreed as it meant pay at double-time. As I was under 18 I was told not to tell anyone. I never did find out who the 'anyone' was.

S. Henderson.

The Furness Abbey Hotel taken around 1910, this was a Furness Railway hotel with 36 rooms, during the 1920s it was the residence of general manager Paul List. *Courtesy of North West Evening Mail.*

This image is included only because it features a rare view of Whinsfield, the mansion located at the top of Cocken Road, long since demolished, it was just north of the railway bridge. The photo was taken at the north end of the works in an area where scrap was emptied from incoming railway wagons. The site in 2016 is occupied by the council household waste tip on Walney Road in an area known to locals as the Dingle.

How it was in 1874, a view of the steelworks from the south from a water colour by George Henry Andrews, an industrial artist commissioned to paint several views of the works.

In the 2015 companion volume to this work a brief mention was made about how Barrow's two heavy industries ran with different cultures. Below is another example recalled by Tony Frankowski a tongsman for many years on the double duo.

"After losing my job because of the works closure in 1983 I secured a position at Barrow shipyard as a plater's helper. In stark contrast to the steelworks I would often find myself stood around in the Assembly shed waiting to be given something to do, needless to say the time dragged! One day I was stood by a pile of scrap steel which was right next to a set of oxy-acetylene burning gear. I set about cutting the scrap into more manageable pieces.

Minutes later my foreman appeared shouting STOP! Or you will have the ruddy caulkers out on strike (I was doing a tradesman's job apparently). I explained that up at the steelworks we didn't have such restrictive practices, burning gear was there for any competent person to use, the mill couldn't wait while someone went looking for a tradesman". Tony Frankowski

The David Caird Foundry (formerly Furness Foundry) on Hindpool Road, Barrow. The two tall cupolas are clearly visible. The firm worked in both haematite iron and haematite steel. Cairds eventually became a casualty of continuous casting - which rendered their ingot moulds obsolete. Photo: courtesy of Roy Chatfield.

Christmas Eve 1964 in Barrow works comptometer office, the girls seem to be in festive spirit.

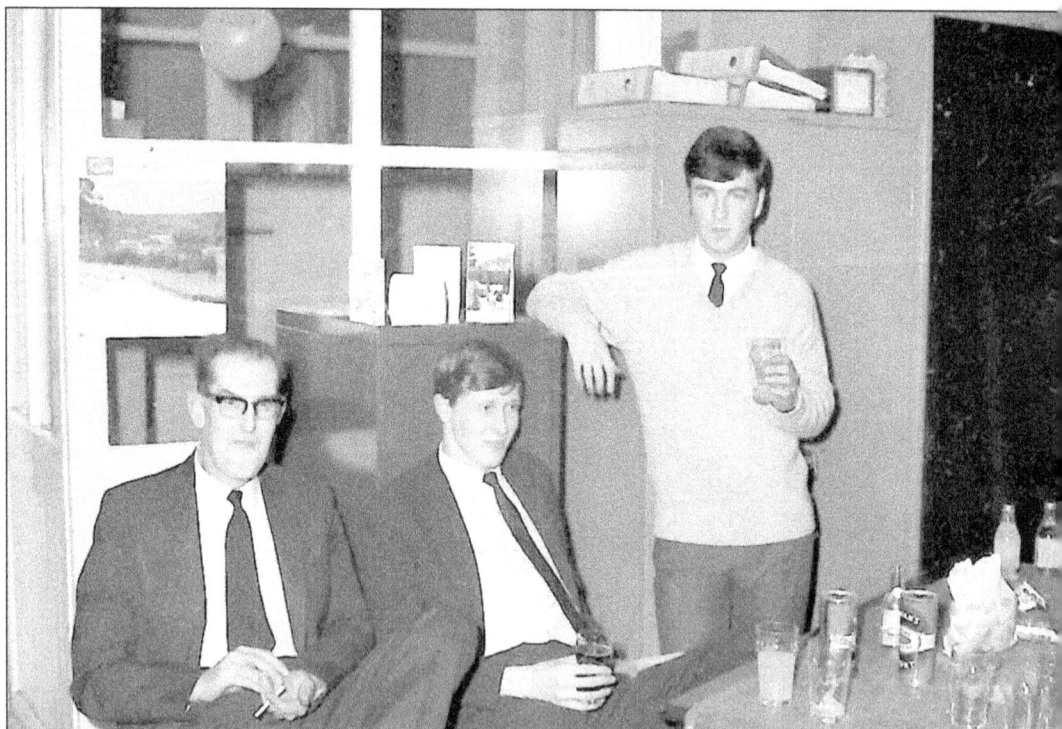

Cost office staff, left to right are Charlie Jackson, John MacCarten and Steve Freeland, Christmas Eve 1969.

Hoop works supremo Maltby Black had a male clerk in the early 1950s who, it was alleged, walked like a penguin. The lads in the mill had christened him 'kipper feet'. Prior to making his daily tour of the mill Mr Black would send kipper feet on a recce. Whenever you spotted the clerk on walkabout you knew the boss would soon follow. Bill Miller, No.3 hoop mill.

Not many people knew this but apparently the ability to play a musical instrument meant that job applications for the steelworks could be fast tracked! I served my time as a millwright on the ironworks side just after the Second World War, I was not happy with the lack of safety measures – it was not unusual to have to shin up the side of a blast furnace with a coil of rope around your neck and tool bag in one hand to reach a valve or similar piece of plant. I therefore made it known that I was after a job in No.2 mill, which meant a good wage and keeping both feet on the ground. I wrote to Jack Charles, labour manager, but found out that the Company didn't like its men defecting to the east (steelworks). Mr Charles sat on my application until a relative with some standing in the steelworks went to see him and told him that I played good cornet." Well why you didn't say earlier", asked the labour manager, "the band needs musicians". Two weeks later I started work in No.2 mill with, also, a place in the works band. (As reported in the *North Western Evening Mail* in September, 1955 the band was renamed Barrow Steelworks Band – originally Barrow Iron & Steelworks Band - by mutual agreement of Messrs Killingbeck and Marple). George Hurley, Blake Street, Hindpool.

Office Canteen Staff, Joan, Margaret and Mima, 10th November, 1967.

My dad recalled a story many times – it obviously left a lasting impression – about the 1930s when he had started in the Analytical Laboratory at the works straight from Barrow Grammar School. Coming off shift, he said, there would often be several school children – many bare-foot and probably from the Scotch Buildings, outside of the gate and begging for food. Men with left-overs from their bait (lunch) would hand it over to them.
Bill Whiteside jnr.

There have been several instances of accidents, in living memory, involving the slag bank loco. The Bowman family recall one in particular. One day in the late 1930s the slag bank loco became a runaway. As can be imagined when coming down the slag bank gradient it was heavily reliant on its braking system, on this particular occasion the brakes failed! Driver George Bowman and his fireman had to take drastic action to avoid catastrophe. Situated at the southern end of Barrow slag bank was a huge pit full of soot which the rail-road passed immediately before levelling out. Having no other option, and in desperation, the two men leapt out as the engine and its empty slag tub jumped the lines on the curve. Minutes later they emerged from the pit looking like Al Jolson impersonators. Having survived the near tragedy the incident made an interesting talking point for weeks in the Bankfield Hotel (situated at the bottom of Teasedale Road, Walney Island). Where George would go, when tidal conditions permitted, via the foot-bridge across Walney channel bed.
Dolly Bowman, Sycamore Grove, Barrow.

Overturned engine after the slag bank incident, courtesy Cumbria Archive and Local studies Centre.

The Barcon mess-room, around 1964, from left to right are – Shift manager Bert Jackson (standing), furnaceman Fred 'Kid' Shepherd, Billy Fell, unknown, unknown, Paddy Coyle, furnaceman Jack Deakin, unknown, mould operators S. Henderson snr., and Jack Johnson, unidentified visitor.

I can remember my father coming home from work, on more than one occasion telling us about the foreign visitors who came to see the new casting process in action. He told us that after one visit in particular the Spanish delegate tried openly to poach him offering a new house together with relocation costs. Some did take these generous offers.

Not everyone at the works were as enthusiastic as others. Alan Howarth of Hood Street, Hindpool, for example voiced his dismay in the local press – the North-West Evening Mail on 12th November, 2013. "If Iain Halliday is our hero he was also something of an anti-hero to people like me and the 600 who lost their jobs because of his invention". Mr Howarth did concede however that the job losses were an indication of the efficiency of the new process and that a rationalisation of the works was necessary. Continuous casting, unlike the processes it supplanted, is not labour intensive.

S. Henderson

Retirement presentation for Bill Pearson. From left to right: Mr T. Marple (seated), Mr J. Lyon, Mr E. Ward (hoop works manager), Iain Halliday (obscured), Bill Pearson, Mr A. Bull, (seated). 4th October, 1963.

Roll Shop circa 1900. This can be seen towards the bottom of the works plan on page 32. The two rolls in the bottom right-hand corner are in the order of 8-tons. Grace's Guides.

Labour manager Mr Ray Carberry at his desk on 14th September, 1966.
Ray had just succeeded Jack Charles.

Works manager Mr E. Aitkin (top) and Barrow Mayor W. M. Gabbut
after giving blood at Barrow works, 14th September, 1966

On the 16th of October, 1959 the *North West Evening Mail* reported that '*Barrow was about to move into its second century*'. The first two blast furnaces – which were constructed in less than ten months – were put into blast on Tuesday, 17th October, 1859. Barrow was about to be wrenched from its rural obscurity. The official opening of Schneider and Hannay's Hindpool plant was on the following day with a special train being laid on to bring guests from Ulverston for the opening.

Fast-forward now one hundred years to October, 1959 and a Dinner and Dance was being held at a Windermere hotel. Managing Director Mr R. B. Sharp, speaking after a dinner of Aylesbury Duck and all the usual accompaniments, said that the event did not mark the centenary of Schneider and Hannay & Co., the Barrow Haematite Steel Company nor Barrow Iron Works Ltd. It was in commemoration of those first furnaces going into production. In stark constrast, the furnaces of today (1959), are charged entirely on imported ores.

View looking east showing the foot-bridge across the bed of Walney Channel. This connected Hindpool with North Scale village, Walney. J. Melville courtesy of Alice Leach.

BARROW IRONWORKS LIMITED

AT THE INVITATION OF
THE CHAIRMAN AND DIRECTORS

CENTENERY
DINNER & DANCE

WINDERMERE HYDRO HOTEL,
BOWNESS-ON-WINDERMERE

FRIDAY, 9TH OCTOBER, 1959

Inside the Splay Shed; an operative is in the process of splaying hoop thereby making cooperage hoop. These would be fitted to white oak barrels by a master Cooper. *Courtesy of D. Howden*

Brady's Leyland Comet articulated wagon emerging from the main entrance loaded with 17-tons of spring steel flatbar. The driver, Tommy Benson from Kendal, is being handed his despatch notes from a work's clerk, circa 1962.
Photo: D. Fisher, details courtesy of Bob Brady.

Barrow's Dwight-Lloyd sinter plant, erected in 1948 by Huntington Heberlin Ltd., during the formation of Barrow Ironworks Ltd., it had a capacity of 60 – 70 tons per hour. This was dismantled and re-erected at the Millom plant in 1967. In the foreground a Fowler diesel hydraulic, also from Barrow, pulls a string of hopper wagons through the Millom works. (Barrow's other diesel loco was a 300hp Hunslett built in 1951). *Photo: Dave Cousins.*

Sunrise over Barrow's slag bank viewed from across Walney channel. It is a ruin just like that of any historic building. And although no longer serving its original purpose, by virtue of its existence it has the ability to make an observer think about its past. It is the only tangible remains of the works on the original site and stands yet to remind us of a once proud industry.

81

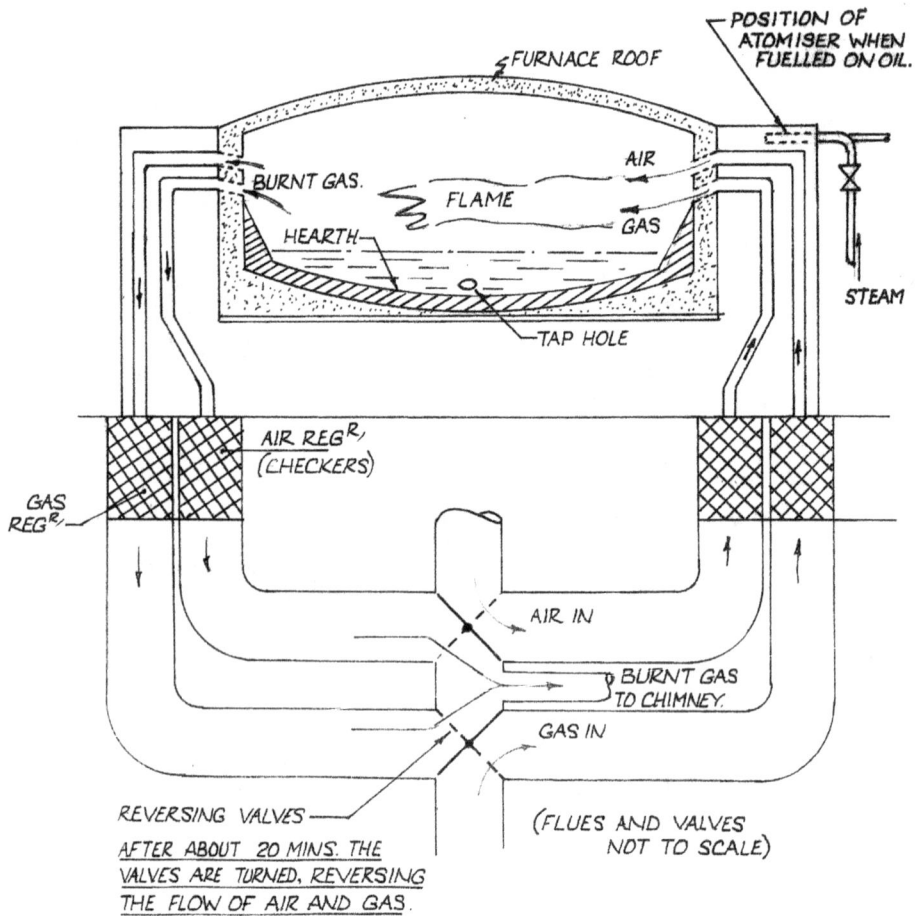

POSITION OF ATOMISER WHEN FUELLED ON OIL.

FURNACE ROOF

BURNT GAS.

AIR

FLAME

GAS

HEARTH

STEAM

TAP HOLE

AIR REG^R, (CHECKERS)

GAS REG^R,

AIR IN

BURNT GAS TO CHIMNEY.

GAS IN

REVERSING VALVES

AFTER ABOUT 20 MINS. THE VALVES ARE TURNED, REVERSING THE FLOW OF AIR AND GAS.

(FLUES AND VALVES NOT TO SCALE)

CROSS-SECTIONAL VIEW OF AN OPEN HEARTH FURNACE WITH, UNDERNEATH, A DIAGRAMMATICAL REPRESENTATION OF REVERSING VALVES, CULVERTS AND FLUES.

S. HENDERSON

Bibliography

Works consulted in preparing this book:

Andrews, M. *The Furness Railway – A History* (Barrai Books, 2012)
Banks, A. G., *H. W. Schneider of Barrow and Bowness* (Kendal: Titus Wilson, 1984)
Barrow Haematite Steel Co., *Barrow Steel, A Brief Survey of Productions* (Ed. J. Burrow & Co. 1937)
Brandt, D. J. O., *The Manufacture of Iron and Steel,* (English Universities Press Ltd. 1953)
Byers, R., *Workington Iron and Steel* (Tempus, 2004)
Campbell, Gifford and Morton Ltd, *Report on Barrow Ironworks, 1962*
Census for England, 1901
Gale, K. *The British Iron and Steel Industry* (David and Charles Ltd.)
Hattersly, R. *The Devonshires,* (Chatto and Windus, 2015)
Henderson, S. and Royall, K. *Barrow Steelworks: an Illustrated History of the Haematite Steel Company.* (The History Press, 2015)
Jackson, Albert, *Steelmaking for Steelmakers,* (United Steel Companies, 1960)
Macfarlane, W., *Iron and Steel Manufacture* (Longmans, Green & Co.)
Marshall, J. D., *Furness and the Industrial Revolution* (B-in-F Library, 1958)
Memorandum on Barrow Ironworks Ltd., 14th March,1960
Report of the visit of the Institution of Mechanical Engineers to Barrow works, 1880, (Grace's Guide)
United Steel Co. Ltd., *This is United Steel,* (United Steel Publicity Dept.1959)

Papers and Periodicals.
Iron and Coal Trades Review, 4 August, 1899
North West Evening Mail. (Various dates)

Barrow News, 24th November, 1961

Barrow Herald, 1st March, 1887

Ibid. 11th March, 1908

Punch, 5th October, 1867

Websites:

Onlinelibrary.wiley.com, The de-nationalisation of the iron and steel industry

Sources by chapter:

Chapter 1: 1880 to 1918

Iron and Coal Trades Review, 4th August 1899

The British Iron and Steel Industry, K. Gale (David and Charles Ltd.)

Iron and Steel Manufacture, W. MacFarlane (Longmans, Green & Co)

The Furness Railway – A History, M. Andrews, 2012.

Report of the visit to Barrow Works by the Institution of Mechanical Engineers, 1880 (Grace's Guides).

Barrow Herald, 1st March 1887.

Ibid. 11th January 1908

onlinelibrary.wiley.com, the de-nationalisation of the Iron and Steel Industry.

Chapter 2: The Inter-War Years

Barrow and District Year Book, 1921.

Barrow Works – A Unique History, James E. Clarke (British Steel Corp.)

The Manufacture of Iron and Steel, D.J.O. Brandt (English Universities Press Ltd., 1953)

This is United Steel, United Steel Publicity Dept., 1959

Barrow Haematite Steel Company, Barrow Steel, A Brief Survey of Productions (Ed J. Burrow & Co., 1937).

Bill Pearson, ex- Barrow Steelworks. Personal communication

Alice Leach, Barrow Civic Society. Personal communication.

Chapter 3: 1942 and United Steel

This is United Steel, United Steel Publicity Dept., 1959

Steelmaking for Steelmakers, A. Jackson.

The Manufacture of Iron and Steel, D.J.O. Brandt (English Universities Press Ltd., 1953)

Billy Fell, ex-Barrow Steelworks, Personal communication.

Bill Pearson, ex-Barrow Steelworks. Personal communication.

Peter Keenan, ex-Barrow Steelworks. Personal communication.

Ray Millard, ex-Barrow Steelworks. Personal communication.

Chapter 4: The Siemens Laboratory

Brian Cubbon, personal communication.

Rodger Bradley, ex-Barrow Steelworks. Personal communication.

Bill Whiteside jnr., personal communication.

Chapter 5: Products

Barrow Haematite Steel Company, Black Book (catalogue) 1936

Ken Law, ex-Barrow Steelworks. Personal communication.

Ray Millard, ex-Barrow Steelworks. Personal communication

Frank Rogan, 4d, Tay Street, Hindpool

Workington Iron and Steel, R. Byers, 2004

Appendices etc.

Hattersly, R. The Devonshires

Dolly Bowman, Personal communication.

Peter Keenan, Personal communication.

George Hurley, Personal communication.

Derek Lyon, Personal communication.

Edwin Whitehead, Personal communication.

Iron and Coal Trades Review, 4th Aug 1899.

Memorandum on Barrow Ironworks Ltd., 14th March, 1960.

North West Evening Mail, 30th March, 1959.

Campbell, Gifford and Morton Ltd, Report on Barrow Ironworks, 1962.

Barrow News, dated Nov 24th 1961

Carl McWhan, personal communication.

Dickens, Charles, Bleak House, Providence Books, 2014.

The Main Man: A. G. Banks, H. W. Schneider of Barrow and Bowness

Bob Brady, personal communication

www.ingramcontent.com/pod-product-compliance
Lightning Source LLC
Chambersburg PA
CBHW081552220326

41598CB00036B/6648